JOSEPHINE MECKSEPER

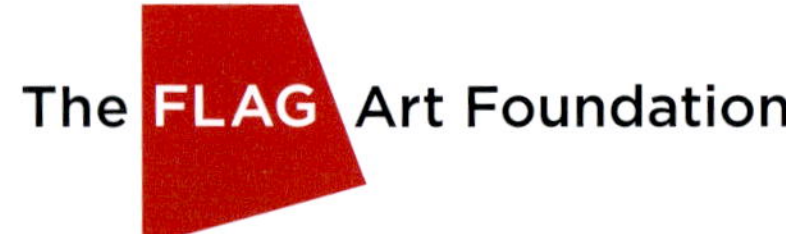

This publication accompanies the exhibition
Josephine Meckseper at The FLAG Art Foundation
February 23-May 26, 2011.

Published by The FLAG Art Foundation 2011
Printed in the USA in a limited edition of 1000

ISBN 978-0-9824315-4-2

The FLAG Art Foundation
545 West 25th Street, 9th Floor
New York, New York 10001
flagartfoundation.org

JOSEPHINE MECKSEPER

Francesco Bonami: Are these monuments to a capitalism of a lesser god?

Josephine Meckseper: Monuments and un-monuments to an entire culture fueled and defined by consumption. Monumental in a sense that they mirror or simulate consumer madness and un-monumental in how they diagnose a cultural pathology that enables wars fought over oil or irreparable environmental damage.

FB: Nothing seems celebratory here; there is always a pathetic aura; pop culture seems to have been replaced by the culture of "poor"—do you agree?

JM: Yes, the mirror-and-chrome sculptures, glass-and-steel vitrines, and mirror slatwalls are not affirmations or glorifications of consumerism. On the contrary, their shiny surfaces are meant as provocations for destruction. They are designed to be targets, like high-end shop windows being smashed during riots and protests. These works mimic retail aesthetics in order to activate the commercial zone into a political one.

FB: Is it then a reflection on how a culture based on luxury turns into "cheapxury" when the economy goes upside down?

JM: It's a rather literal reflection since there is no escape for the viewer because of the many mirrored surfaces in this exhibition. The works also reference the car dealerships in Chelsea that are defined by a specific aesthetic based on chrome and bargain deals and a lack of real values that further eroded during the financial crisis. Chain drugstores like Duane Reade use the same mirrored slatwalls to sell discounted toothpaste or cosmetics.

FB: What are the politics within the work?

JM: On one side is a (post-)Marxist critique on the fetishization of the object; on the other, a new history of the object that has become a free agent and is now arranging and rearranging reality for us. Similarly, as on television, where news and advertisements blend seamlessly into one other, the artwork, a product with symbolic and commercial value, is held hostage in a vicious cycle.

FB: Are these ghosts of Jasper Johns's flags?

JM: Johns is in some ways a cultural referent in my work, an American icon or emblem as much as General Motors or the White House.

FB: Some of the works look like Joseph Beuys's vitrines. But while Beuys's were shrines to the remains of performance and action, yours seem to be shrines to the remains of the rite of consumption.

JM: The three vitrines in the exhibition capture the sense of cultural performance in consumption. Consumption in a larger sense includes the digestion of art and images. One vitrine houses a photograph taken at the Emirates Palace in Abu Dhabi a few months ago. It shows a Giacometti sculpture in front of a Daniel Buren painting. There is no allusion to where the image was taken; the location and purpose of the image become casualties of global indifference. The consumer performance aspect is further exemplified in the form of a taxidermy black crow holding a piece of jewelry in its beak as if caught shoplifting in midflight; or dishes, Pepsi cans, and scrubbers stuck on metal poles like sinister totems of a mad consumer society.

FB: While Cady Noland's work is about some kind of suburban nomadism, your work feels like the nomad subject has been stuck somewhere and has nowhere to go. The frontier is within our shopping mall.

JM: Cady Noland is addressing a specific American cultural pathology in her work in a genius way. My subjects are the more global psychopaths who find themselves trapped in a megamall in Dubai, for example, where all the cultural referents are borrowed and mirrored indefinitely until the oil runs out and the next megamall in another country becomes the new frontier.

FB: Can one think of the work as an archaeology of a shopping age?

JM: These works are, in a sense, time capsules for a near and far future. They represent everything that is wrong with our culture and a possible end phase of an expanding global capitalism that may or may not be sustainable in a few decades. They are dubious souvenirs of our time.

FB: The vitrines remind me of Warhol Time Capsules.

JM: The cardboard boxes Andy Warhol filled in his time anthologized culture in a literal way. My vitrines similarly function as containers and entrapments. Except that the cultural fragments I am chronicling are more sinister and less digestible because of their focus on the end points of cultural production and their political mechanisms. They are open modern-day sarcophagi with remnants of our civilization on display.

FB: Haim Steinbach's work has a bourgeois aspect to it. Some kind of compulsive order. Your work seems to have gone beyond order and compulsion into the dysfunctional realm of the celebration of subluxury.

JM: My work borrows its aesthetics more directly from retail environments and is less invested in the "artistic" translation of its stereotypes. It's a more open-ended process in which different forms such as window display, mirror platform, photography, and film resist any real categorization.

FB: Is the wheel sculpture a possible "Detroit memorial" for a time when the car was at the center of U.S. economy and culture?

JM: It is an example of a specific (male) cultural icon that is now deteriorating in front of our eyes. Ironically, I made the wheel sculpture just a few months before the financial collapse in 2008 and a year before General Motors declared bankruptcy.

FB: Could you imagine the shopping mall as some kind of real-time museum of the consumption of culture?

JM: The mall has become the ultimate American landscape. It is the modern epicenter of artificial leisure and activity, a new church and museum at once. Everything is on display: commodities, entertainment, military recruiting, and exploitation of the work force.

FB: There is nothing biographical in this work, right?

JM: My work follows a butterfly-net principle. It catches cultural signifiers and freezes them into immobile objects. A Chinese counterfeit designer, for example, could come up with very similar products and concepts.

FB: The shop window is going to disappear in the future; the new window is the Web window. Do you see your work as some kind of nostalgic representation of the physicality of the street window, its capacity to break up the urban flow and structure? The end of Walter Benjamin's Arcades?

JM: The manifestation and aesthetics of consumption are in a state of complete transition. The face of capitalism is getting a total makeover. In Europe, you can still find shop window decorations that have remained the same for several decades. There is a timelessness and romanticism in the look of specialty stores that sell items such as orthopedic shoes. In a few decades no one will remember these stores. The new flâneur is an Internet junkie like the characters in the *South Park* episode "Make Love, Not Warcraft," so glued to the screen that they don't even bother to go to the bathroom when they have diarrhea. It's a rather unromantic future.

ENTER THE DRAGON

BY JOHN CASSIDY

In the late eighteenth century, the inhabitants of Great Britain were drinking so much tea from imperial China that a big trade deficit had arisen between the two countries. China demanded payment in silver, which was putting pressure on the Exchequer and the pound sterling. Eager to find a product that the Chinese would import, the English settled on opium, which was produced in parts of India that they controlled. In 1773, the governor-general of Bengal broke up the local opium-smuggling cartel and granted the London-based East India Company a monopoly, which endured for more than fifty years. During the next five decades, China's annual imports of British-supplied opium went from seventy-five tons to nine hundred.

The rulers of imperial China took exception to this development, which was turning millions of their subjects into shiftless dope fiends. They tried banning the import of opium, to little effect. Finally, in 1839, a commissioner of the Canton region clamped down on the illegal trade, forcing British merchants to hand over thousands of chests of opium, and sent Queen Victoria a letter declaring, "We mean to cut off this harmful drug forever." In London, there was outrage. Rather than negotiate with China, Lord Palmerston, the Foreign Secretary, dispatched a naval flotilla.

Confronted with iron-hulled steamships and powerful cannons, the Chinese military was hopelessly outmatched; the British seized control of Canton and the surrounding areas, killing thousands. Palmerston and his allies loftily insisted that the intervention was in the service of broader British interests and of the principle of free trade, which London was promoting throughout the Empire. The *Times* of London nonetheless dubbed the conflict the Opium War, and the young William Ewart Gladstone, in one of his early parliamentary speeches, said that the British flag "is become a pirate flag, to protect an infamous traffic."

In 1842, the Chinese government was forced to sign the Treaty of Nanking, promising Britain more than twenty million silver dollars in reparations (around half a billion dollars in today's currency), minimal tariffs on its goods, docking rights at five Chinese ports, and sovereignty over Hong Kong. Fifteen years later, complaining of trade impediments, France, Russia, and the United States, all of which had growing business interests in the Far East, joined the British in a second Opium War. Under the terms of the Convention of Peking, in 1860, China agreed to open up more of its ports to foreign exporters, to pay more in reparations, to allow British ships to transport indentured Chinese laborers ("coolies") to the United States, and to legalize the opium trade. The country's economic subjugation—the Chinese Communists later referred to the period as the "century of humiliation"—may have ultimately helped bring down the Qing dynasty and usher in civil war and revolution. But it certainly cleared up Britain's trade deficit.

Today, of course, China can't be pushed around as easily. Many observers foresee a coming clash of civilizations between an economically vibrant yet politically illiberal developing world, led by China, and a slow-growing democratic West. "China poses the most serious challenge to the United States since the half-century Cold War struggle with the Soviet Union," Stefan Halper, a veteran foreign-policy expert, writes in his book *The Beijing Consensus: How China's Authoritarian Model Will Dominate the Twenty-first Century.*

Note the word *model* in the subtitle of Halper's book. The elements of this model, in most accounts, include keeping key areas of the economy under state ownership or state control; using government subsidies and currency manipulation to promote exports; setting up sovereign wealth funds to buy companies and influence in the West; and making backdoor deals with equally autocratic states to insure access to oil and other natural resources. In all of this, the unifying theme is a reliance on the guiding hand of the state rather than on private decisions made in the marketplace. In *The End of the Free Market: Who Wins the War Between States and Corporations?,* Ian Bremmer, the president of the economic consultancy firm Eurasia Group, writes that, until recently, "private wealth, private investment, and private enterprise appeared to have carried the day. But as the sun sets on the first decade of the twenty-first century, that story has already become ancient history. The power of the state is back"—and back in a way that "threatens free markets and the future of the global economy."

To be sure, the astonishing transformation since China adopted, in 1978, what Deng Xiaoping described as "socialism with Chinese characteristics" poses a big challenge to Western ideas about politics and about economics—but it is important to distinguish between the two. In promoting the development of a dynamic, competitive economy within the confines of a one-party state, the descendants of Chairman Mao seem to have arrived at a new social contract that says to the governed: Go and engage with the global economy, set up businesses, invest, make as much money as you can, but leave the politics to us. From a Jeffersonian perspective, what's going on may look like repressive regimes foisting unpopular policies on peoples striving to be free. But, as Halper, who served in the Nixon, Ford, and Reagan Administrations, points out, these policies enjoy a good deal of popular support. "Given a choice between market democracy and its freedoms and market authoritarianism and its high growth, stability, improved living standards, and limits on expression—a majority in the developing world and in many middle-sized, non-Western powers prefer the authoritarian model," Halper writes. If this unsettling trend isn't arrested in the coming decades, he adds, "the United States will be left in a world unsympathetic to the democratic values and principles that have guided Western progress for more than two centuries."

That may be overstating the case. History suggests that "market authoritarianism" is often a transitional stage of development. During the 1970s and '80s, a number of Southeast Asian countries employed it to drag themselves out of poverty. Today, South Korea, Thailand, and Indonesia are democracies, of sorts. Singapore, on the other hand, remains essentially a one-party city-state. Who can say for sure which of these paths Russia (already a democracy, albeit a distinctly curtailed one) and China will end up following?

Despite recent developments, China, in particular, is still a pretty poor place, with a per capita GDP of about three thousand dollars in 2008. By 2050, according to a recent study from the Carnegie Endowment, this figure will rise to about thirty-three thousand dollars, which would place China roughly where Spain is today. It is hard to disagree with George Magnus, an economic adviser to UBS Investment Bank, when he says, in his new book, *Uprising: Will Emerging Markets Shape or Shake the World Economy,* that "some sort of change in China is inevitable"—that, "sooner or later, rising living standards and the spread of modernity through the country are going to generate a growing public clamor for political participation and institutional reform."

In the economic realm, many analysts have fundamentally misrepresented the Western pattern of development. The closer you look at how countries such as Britain and the United States became prosperous, the less you see of *laissez-faire* and the more you see of government intervention. Lord Palmerston's "gunboat diplomacy" in defense of the opium trade may have been an especially bald version of state capitalism, but the basic strategy of enlisting state power in pursuit of commercial advantage, and vice versa, has been anything but the exception. Far from subverting the Western way of doing business, the developing world is, at last, stealing some of its tricks.

Take free trade. Even before 1791, when Alexander Hamilton published his famous "Report on the Subject of Manufactures," Congress used tariffs to protect favored industries. During the War of 1812, which was precipitated in part by trade disputes, it doubled import duties on manufactured goods, to 25 percent. Abraham Lincoln raised them again, to roughly 50 percent. Ha-Joon Chang, an economist at the University of Cambridge, has observed that Lincoln, revered as the Great Emancipator, "might equally be labeled the great protector—of American manufacturing."

During the half century after Lincoln's presidency, the business-backed Republican Party was in power for most of the time, and tariffs on manufactured goods remained at 40 to 50 percent, the highest levels anywhere. It was during these years that the U.S. economy grew to rival the economies of Britain and Germany in industries such as iron and steel and chemicals—all of which benefited from protection. "Free trade economists have to explain how free trade can be an explanation for the economic success of today's rich countries," Chang notes, "when it simply had not been practiced very much before they became rich."

China, Korea, and other rising economies are often reproached for using government money and influence to bolster home industries to the disadvantage of foreign competitors, a practice that is known as "industrial policy," and is frowned on by international trade law. Such discriminatory policies are also referred to as dirigisme—a clue that the concept didn't originate in the Far East. After the Second World War, the government of France's Fifth Republic created "national champions" in strategic areas of the French economy, such as transportation, energy, and aerospace. The policy gave rise to big companies like Air France, the French railway operator SNCF, the utility company EDF, and the aeronautics contractor EADS, all of which are partly or wholly owned by the French government.

But industrial policy long predates General de Gaulle. In 1791, Alexander Hamilton proposed a series of policies to help transform America into an industrial economy, including export subsidies, prizes for industrial inventions, and public investment in infrastructure. During and after the Civil War, the federal government, by providing generous land grants and cheap financing, was instrumental in opening up the Great Plains and directing the expansion westward. The Central Pacific and Union Pacific railroads were both government-chartered companies that benefited from large land grants, not to mention vast sums in government loans.

U.S. industrial policy may be less visible these days, but it still plays a key role in maintaining our competitive edge. Much of this assistance comes through the Pentagon, which, by paying for research-and-development projects that private investors would be reluctant to finance, has helped to create three of our biggest export industries: commercial aircraft, military aircraft, and computers. The Boeing 747 and many other modern jetliners were developed from designs for military aircraft. Fairchild Semiconductor, which helped pioneer the development of the silicon transistor, in the 1950s, was a military contractor, as were many other technology firms that helped launch the modern computer industry, such as Texas Instruments. And, famously, the Internet was created by the Pentagon's Defense Advanced Research Projects Agency (DARPA), which continued to operate it until 1990.

Then there's the financial sector. Developing Asian countries have been criticized for propping up struggling banks rather than allowing market forces to operate. During the recent financial crisis, of course, the United States—along with other prominent members of the World Trade Organization, like Britain and Germany—found itself doing precisely the same thing. As for the U.S. bailouts of General Motors and Chrysler, a case can be made that they violated WTO rules, not that anybody is going to call Washington to account. Compared with these naked exercises in industrial policy, some of the Chinese infractions that have most exercised the WTO seem relatively minor. In the first half of 2010, General Motors' Chinese subsidiary, which is a joint venture with Chinese manufacturers, sold more than a million cars and trucks, a jump of almost 50 percent over 2009. For the first time, the Detroit automaker sold more cars in China than it did in the United States.

Both Bremmer and Halper devote considerable space to China's recent efforts to secure its future supplies of energy and natural resources, which have involved cozying up to repressive regimes in places like Zimbabwe, Sudan, and Iran. "The use of oil, gas, and other commodities as political tools and strategic assets," Bremmer writes, "can be an essential part of state capitalism," and he notes that three-quarters of the world's oil reserves are owned by national oil companies. There is no disputing that securing access to natural resources is a major strategic objective in foreign policy, but that's equally true of Western countries and their developing rivals. During the late nineteenth century, tales of diamonds, gold, and other precious minerals in limitless quantities helped spark the Scramble for Africa. After the First World War, Britain and the United States, conscious of the future importance of the Persian Gulf's vast oil reserves, helped install a series of pliable desert monarchs who granted access to Western oil companies on favorable terms. In 1953, two years after Mohammad Mosaddegh, the democratically elected prime minister of Iran, nationalized the British-owned Anglo-Iranian Oil Company, the CIA helped organize a successful coup against him. Needless to say, the United States continues to stabilize "friendly" oil-exporting governments, like the Kingdom of Saudi Arabia and the Sultanate of Oman, with extensive military and technical assistance.

The heavy hand of American domestic and foreign policy in shaping economic outcomes tends to get ignored in current policy debates, in which economic issues are usually cast in ideological terms, devoid of their historical context. However, there are some encouraging signs of revisionism. In a recent book, *The Great Betrayal,* Clyde Prestowitz, a former U.S. trade negotiator who founded the Washington-based Economic Strategy Institute, includes a chapter on "How America Really Got Rich." And in the book *Losing Control: The Emerging Threats to Western Prosperity,* Stephen D. King, the chief economist at HSBC, the London-based global bank, notes, "Western governments have used the methods of state capitalism for hundreds of years in their bid to shape the world around them. . . . The idea that market forces alone led to the West's success is nonsense."

Unfortunately, in policy circles—and among much of the general public—the old mantras about the free market and private enterprise continue to dominate. In seeking to broaden access to private health insurance, the Obama administration was accused of plotting a takeover of the entire health-care industry. In cutting taxes and boosting federal spending to avert a depression, it was accused of embracing socialism. Even supposedly serious economists lend support to these views, arguing that the dysfunctional health-care industry is best left to its own devices, or that the eight-hundred-billion-dollar stimulus program has had virtually no impact on jobs and on GDP This is what comes of forgetting the critical role that states have played in nurturing, protecting, and financing their industries, as well as in taxing and taming them. The greatest danger that Western prosperity now faces isn't posed by any Beijing consensus; it's posed by the myth of the free market.

DEMOLITION

BY JAMES FREY

Crashed.
Recovered.
Crashed.
Recovered.
Crashed.
Recovered
Crashed.
Crashed.
Crashed.
Each time.
The rich hedged.
The poor stayed poor.
The middle got destroyed.
Each time.
The rich got richer.
The poor stayed poor.
And their numbers grew.
Detroit.
Cleveland.
Buffalo
Baltimore.
Crumbling.
Deserted.
Warzones.
Philadelphia.
Miami.
Atlanta.
Memphis.
Heavily.
Armed.
Citizens.
New York.
Los Angeles.
Walled.
Neighborhoods.
Chicago.
Seattle.
Shrinking.
Police forces.
Boston.
Dallas.
Houston.
New Orleans.
One side.
Has.
Oakland.
Las Vegas.
One side.
Not.
Unrest.

Riots.
Burning buildings.
Stores.
Cars.
Schools.
Burning hospitals.
Burning bodies.

Government forces surrounded the fires.
And let them burn.
And when all that was left was ash.
They left.
Containment became policy.
Let them burn their homes and kill themselves if that's what they want to do.
There is no money to rebuild.
And it's not the government's responsibility.
To tame animals.
Crashed.
Crashed.
Crashed.

Spectacle.
Is an escape.
For those who watch it.
It removes them from reality.
Gives them pleasure.
For a minute or an hour, it doesn't matter.
For those who participate.
It provides an opportunity.
The greater the risk.
The greater the reward.
For those who have nothing.
Risk is meaningless.
As the disparity grew.
The walls grew.
The fires grew.
The spectacles grew.
It wasn't enough to watch them killing each other on the news.
Or the internet.
It wasn't enough to watch them die in the streets.
Hungry dirty and penniless.
Team sports disappeared.
The mobs that descended on stadiums became uncontrollable.
Combat sport rose.
Cage fights.
Ring fights.
Pits.
No rules.
Weapons.
One on one.
Two on two.

Six in a ring every person for himself.
Twenty-five in a Battle Royale.
Men.
Women.
Starting at twelve years old.
Anyone could fight.
Anyone could win.
The prizes varied.
A vehicle.
Health insurance.
A home in a safe neighborhood.
A college scholarship for a child.
A year's supply of food.
Cash.
At first the fights ended with unconsciousness or surrender.
People lived to fight again.
But the viewers wanted more than blood.
Screamed for it.
Were willing to pay for it.
They wanted permanence.
They wanted an end.
They wanted everything.

A new stadium was built.
Away.
From crowds.
From cities.
The inaugural event.
A Demolition Derby.
Thirty drivers.
Thirty cars.
Parked around the edges.
Engines running.
Go.
Drive.
Attack or avoid.
Driver's choice.
When the cars died.
The drivers went on.
Until they died.
No rules.
No stopping.
Until the end.
Five hundred thousand dollars for the winner.
Cremation for everyone else.
Five thousand people applied.
Each with their own car.
Each with their own reason.
Each with their own idea.
Of how they'd make it out.
Or not.
They were screened.
Examinied.
Given psychological testing.

Chosen for their hunger.
Their rage.
Their capacity for cruelty.
Thirty drivers.
Thirty cars.
Money.
Cremation.

In their glittering towers.
Behind their walls.
They gathered.
With popcorn.
And soda.
Wings.
And beer.
Cheese.
And wine.
Expectations.
Desire.
Thirst.
Their screens filled with the steel.
Drivers.
The roar.
Each car numbered.
Each driver with the number on their back.
Names don't matter.
Families.
Histories.
Debts.
Or reasons.
They're just number.
On their car.
And on their back.

It starts with a gunshot.
The Master of the Derby.
A rifle.
A scope.
A number chosen at random.
Crosshairs on the number's forehead.
A big surprise to kick it off.
Bullet in the brain.
Back of the head blown off.
A chance at the big bucks over before it started.
Boohoo, said the viewers at home, as they howled with glee.
Boohoo said the other contestants.
Boohoo said the Master.
Boo fucking hoo.

And so it began.
Metal.
Gas.
Blood.
Death.
Delight.

Car flipped driver crushed.
Car against wall rammed repeatedly steel shards from the door impale.
Gastank boom.
Gastank boom.
Gastank boom.
Two burn inside one got out burned on the concrete.
Head-on collision both expected to make it neither does.
The Master chose another number.
Bullet in the brain.
Back of the head blown off.
Car died, driver's bold, pulled another out and broke neck, took car.
Car died, driver's bold, ran for another, hit run over, tires across spine, spine shattered.
Car died, driver waited, smart move, until the others saw, ganged up, gastank boom.
Tactics emerged, strategies.
Strike with the rear of your car, does more damage to opponent, less to driver
Hit just ahead of the front wheels and take out the radiator
Hit the back wheels take out the drive train.
Head-on shots bend frames, angled shots protect them.
Keep the drivers door near the wall.
Accelerate into a shot, accelerate out.

Don't stay in the car if it dies, the only chance is to kill and get another.
The field dwindles.
Twenty two.
Eighteen.
Fifteen.
Some deaths mundane.
Another crushing against another wall.
Some spectacular.
Two drivers without cars met in the center one decapitated the other with a shard of glass.
Eleven.
Nine.
Seven.
Driver tried to fix tire got his neck driven over.
Car flipped driver crawled out legs didn't work, didn't work, another driver slowly drove up said legs,
    up back, over head, head exploded.
Four.
Three.
Two hours of action.
Metal.
Gas.
Blood.

Death.
Delight.
Three drivers left.
Cars dead.
Two of them soon to join.
Viewers watched
Waited.
Hard.
Wet.
Nervous.
Scared.

Overjoyed.
Drivers sat.
No one moved.
Fifteen minutes.
Thirty.
Master drew another number.
Boom.
Bullet in the brain.
Back of the head blown off.
Two.
They emerged.
Climbed out the windows.
Looked for weapons.
Viewers.
Gathered together.
Waited
Popcorn soda wings beer cheese and wine.
Expectations.
Desire.
Thirst.
Hard.
Wet.
Two left.
Walked towards each other.
Slowly.
Walked.
Five hundred thousand.
To breathe.
To eat.
To live.
Enough to escape.
Hard.
Wet.
Walked towards each other.
Slowly.

RETHINKING THE POLITICAL ECONOMY OF POWER

BY STEPHEN ROACH

History is replete with painful examples of the lemming-like character of economies and financial markets. Irrespective of any danger, they run together until the end. That's especially the case during booms. A deeply entrenched political economy of power—dominated by elected officials, policy makers, regulators, and captains of industry—makes it exceedingly difficult to change course until it's too late. Rare is the enlightened system that does so on its own. Invariably, it takes a crisis to force the power structure to rethink the core value propositions of economic stewardship.

The Great Crisis of 2008–09 is an obvious and important case in point. It was, by far, the worst financial and economic crisis in modern history, and yet the authorities were asleep at the switch as it all unfolded. The 545-page report of the Financial Crisis Inquiry Commission—a bipartisan investigatory body empowered by the U.S. Congress to get to the bottom of this mess—puts an important part of the blame squarely on ideology. The Commission concluded that America's once-disciplined system—its financial markets as well as its economy—had been hijacked by a reckless mind-set of self-regulation. Seduced by an unprecedented boom, a broad consensus of Americans came to believe that ever-powerful markets—operating through the all-knowing invisible hand—could handle anything and everything.

Maybe not. Autopilot was, in fact, the last thing America needed as it raced toward the abyss. Yet the boom obliterated any semblance of responsible stewardship. Denial was widespread—from Wall Street, to the ratings agencies, to the alphabet soup of Washington regulators (SEC, FED, FDIC, OCC, CFTC, etc.), to the so-called congressional oversight function, itself. The common thread that tied it all together was a culture of excess that would stop at nothing to rationalize and perpetuate a false prosperity.

Yes, in the end, that's exactly what it was—a false prosperity. U.S. economic growth rested on an increasingly shaky foundation of speculative bubbles—first dot-com stocks and then residential property. But that wasn't enough. To pull it off, America also needed a credit bubble—cheap and open-ended financing that would enable the seemingly costless extraction of capital gains from fantasy-like increases in asset values. The power structure—from Washington to Wall Street—was more than happy to comply.

With the benefit of hindsight, it is easy to point fingers at those who were especially derelict in their responsibility. The Financial Crisis Inquiry Commission offers up many suspects. Wall Street, of course, is high on the list—and deservedly so. But so, too, is a long string of public officials, with former Fed Chairman Alan Greenspan leading the way. While the Maestro (aka Mr. Greenspan) certainly did play a key role in all this, I would be the first to concede that isn't the real point.

Greenspan personified the ideological tilt toward self-regulation. As an apostle of Ayn Rand, a leading *laissez-faire* objectivist, he believed that markets always knew best. While markets could make mistakes from time to time, Greenspan believed in a Humpty-Dumpty-like role for central banks—sweeping in after disruptions and crises and putting the broken pieces of a damaged system back together again.

Never mind that the pieces were all but vaporized in the aftermath of the Great Crisis—that the hands-off mantra of self-regulation was totally out of step with the inevitably lethal combination of complexity (i.e., financial derivatives) and interconnectedness (i.e., the cross-border linkages of globalization). The far deeper question is, Why? Why did the body politic need to lionize a Maestro and condone such excesses in the first place?

The answer can be found in the inner sanctum of America's culture of excess—the interplay between power, prosperity, and politics. It starts with politics. By definition, there is a pronounced myopia to a political system with a two-year election cycle. Election campaigns are waged on the basis of results that have been delivered—or not delivered—over a very short period of time. Meanwhile, there is a deeply entrenched inertia to the U.S. political power structure: Since 1980, fully 95 percent of all incumbents who stood for re-election in the House of Representatives have been returned to office. It follows that short-term results—in the economics sphere, next quarter's GDP and unemployment—are all that matter for reelection and maintaining a grip on power. An analogous perspective applies to equally myopic financial and corporate power brokers—next quarter's earnings are the only thing that seems to count.

As seen through that lens, the siren song of the boom becomes almost impossible to resist. When the short-term stars were in seemingly perfect alignment, as they certainly appeared to be in the four years before the Subprime Crisis, the political and financial power structure only wanted more. And it was rewarded for delivering just that. There was little or no incentive to question the rosy outcome. Never mind the strong undercurrent of complacency. The hopes and dreams of the ultimate virtuous cycle had taken on a life of their own.

Aided and abetted by the ideology of self-regulation, the final phase of the boom was especially seductive. Yet in an increasingly complex and interconnected world, the lack of adult supervision was a recipe for disaster. America's bubble-dependent economy was an accident waiting to happen. When the bubbles burst—as they always do—the ensuing implosion, and the economic carnage it unleashed, did not escape the wrath of the American electorate. Just 87 percent of the incumbents who stood for reelection were returned to office in the House in the midterm elections of 2010—still an amazingly high percentage, but in fact, the lowest incumbency-return ratio since 1970 and a rejection that was strong enough to result in a stunning loss of control for the Democrats in the House of Representatives.

Notwithstanding this unusually strong message from the electorate, political myopia remains an enduring feature of the post-crisis climate. Washington not only ignored the perils of an increasingly unstable boom but it has subsequently rushed in after the fact with a classic quick fix timed to placate voters before the midterm elections of November 2010. In one of the more glaring disconnects in recent history, the U.S. Congress passed the Dodd-Frank Bill—a major re-regulation of the financial system—*before* it heard back from its own Financial Crisis Inquiry Commission as to what actually caused the great implosion of 2008–09.

Surely there must be a better way for the power structure to exercise responsible stewardship of the American system. The short-term spoils of political and financial power have instilled a deep reluctance to take up vitally important items on the long-term agenda—challenges such as deficit reduction, competitiveness, educational reform, climate change, and retirement income security. Instead, ever-myopic and increasingly polarized U.S. politicians are far more inclined to focus on the here and now and "kick the can down the road"—leaving the heavy lifting of solving tough problems for the proverbial next generation of leaders and citizens. As America clamors more and more for instant gratification, the value proposition that has long underpinned the U.S. political system gets turned inside out. And by electing representatives with false promises, the insidious nature of this self-delusion only deepens.

If there is one clear message from the Great Crisis, it is that America can no longer afford to stay this reckless course. The political economy of power is in need of a fundamental realignment. It wouldn't be the first time. Twice earlier during the post–World War II era the U.S. Congress enacted landmark legislation that redefined the rules of engagement for the economic and financial power structure. In both cases, each of these adjustments benefited from the political will that typically gets mustered in the aftermath of crises. In 1946, Congress passed the so-called Full Employment Act. Seared by the painful memory of an unemployment rate that hit 25 percent in the depths of the Great Depression, Washington vowed to set policy with an aim toward achieving maximal growth in employment. And in 1978, with the U.S. in the throes of a debilitating inflation, Congress enacted the Humphrey-Hawkins Act, which added price stability to Washington's policy mandate.

While this "dual mandate"—full employment and price stability—worked reasonably well for about twenty years, it obviously failed to prevent the Great Crisis. And so the mandate needs to be changed once again—this time, with an aim toward protecting financial and economic stability. Never again should a mindset of self-regulation be allowed to condone a reckless interplay between asset and credit bubbles on the one hand and an asset- and debt-dependent real economy on the other. It will take nothing short of a new accountability of the body politic—underscored by the hardwiring of a financial stability mandate into the legally binding compact between Congress and policy makers—to break the daisy chain. Only then would the authorities have the political cover they need to address the perils of a false prosperity that can arise from ever-precarious asset and credit bubbles.

On this count, the United States may actually have a good deal to learn from China—the world's newly ascendant power, which was remarkably successful in tempering the aftershocks of the Great Crisis. China's success was due, in large part, to aggressive actions—before, during, and after the crisis—that were taken to ensure financial and economic stability. The centerpiece of this effort—a massive fiscal stimulus in late 2008—had little or none of the cumbersome implementation lags that bogged down comparable efforts in the developed world. With its economy deteriorating sharply in the immediate aftermath of the crisis, state-directed China acted first—and asked questions later.

The Chinese comparison invites an even deeper examination of the role of the state in shaping growth and prosperity. At the core of China's miracle of the past thirty years has been an export-led mercantilist development model, resting firmly on the twin pillars of industrial policy (picking the sectors that are winners and losers) and currency suppression. This, of course, is the same recipe followed by Japan—Asia's first miracle of the post–World War II era. As two "lost decades" suggest, however, the Japanese approach was deeply flawed. By focusing on stability—financial, economic, and, ultimately, social stability—China may well have learned the most important lessons of Japan's monstrous bubbles and the spectacular failure they spawned. This message should not be lost on the United States—or even on Europe, for that matter.

Putting a high priority on stability would represent a fundamental change in America's rules of the game. Significantly, it would entail a reworking of the social contract that lies at the heart of this nation's culture of power. That's because stability would require greater policy discipline during times of froth. That, in turn, raises the distinct possibility that economies and financial markets might have to forsake short-term gains for longer-term sustainability. For a growth-fixated power structure, such a reprioritization could result in the ultimate comeuppance—the need to accept a growth sacrifice as a cost for maintaining stability. Yet how else can an otherwise undisciplined system avoid the temptations and risks of a false prosperity?

A deeply entrenched political system will undoubtedly resist. After all, tough medicine—and the growth sacrifice it might entail—is tantamount to incumbency risk for a nation with a two-year election cycle. For the Washington power structure, that could well be a very bitter pill to swallow. That underscores one of the most troubling aspects of the current post-crisis climate: Unlike in earlier periods of major economic and financial stress, when a sense of shared sacrifice was both understood and accepted, today's America seems to be lacking in the political will that is needed to face up to its toughest challenges.

The Great Crisis suggests it is high time for the United States to start taking its medicine. As the results of the 2010 midterm elections imply, a lingering post-crisis carnage means that incumbents finally need to confront their myopia. Otherwise, they will be confronted with a succession of ever-deepening crises. And the powerful will then become the powerless.

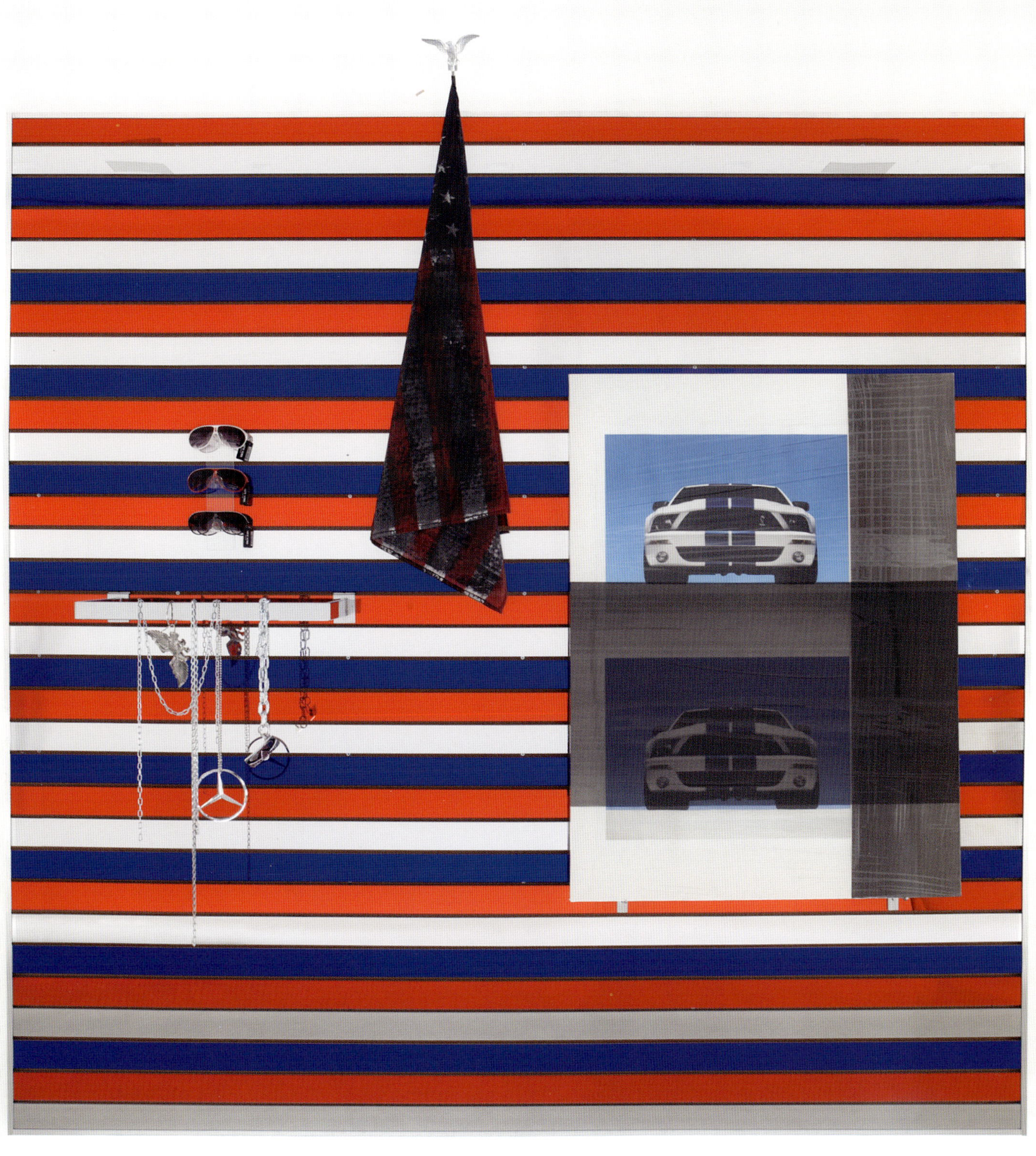

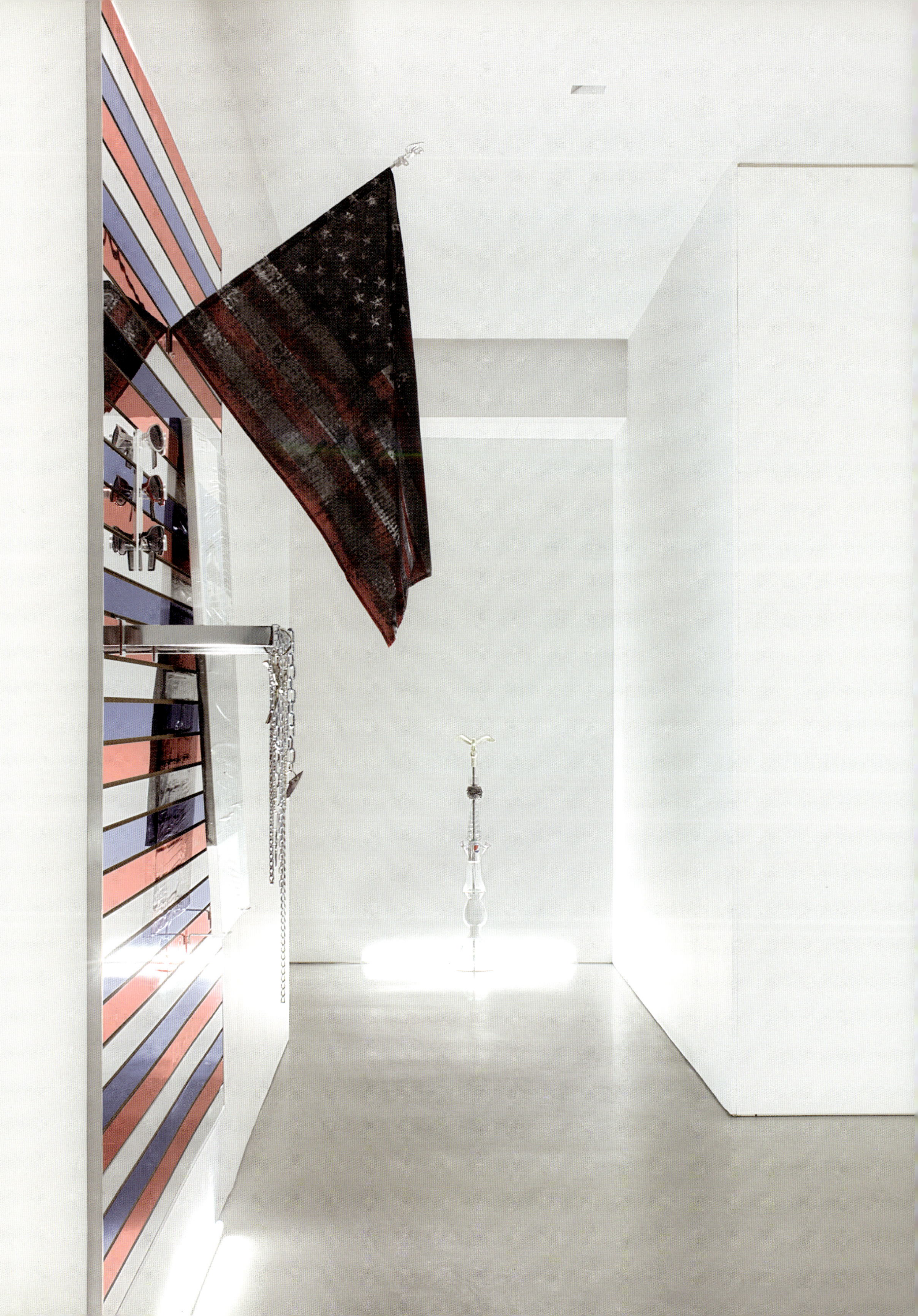

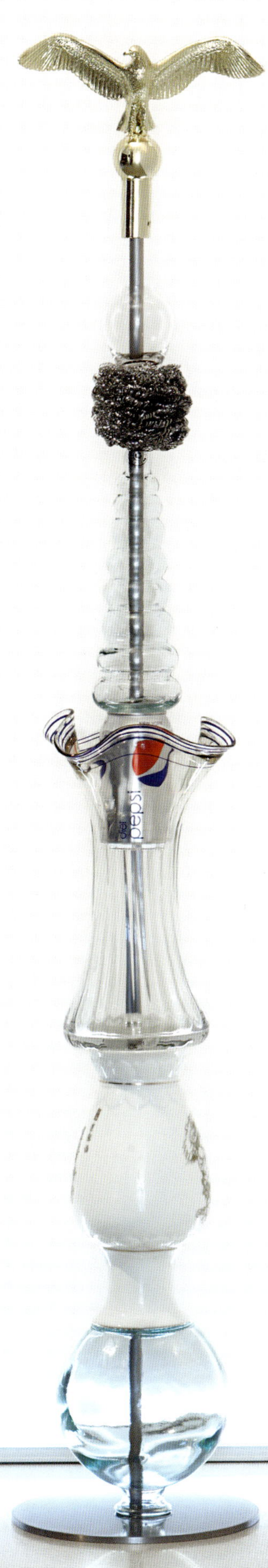

Diet
Coke
Diet
Join Diet Coke in support of
women's heart health programs.*
Visit www.dietcoke.com.
THE
heart
355 mL

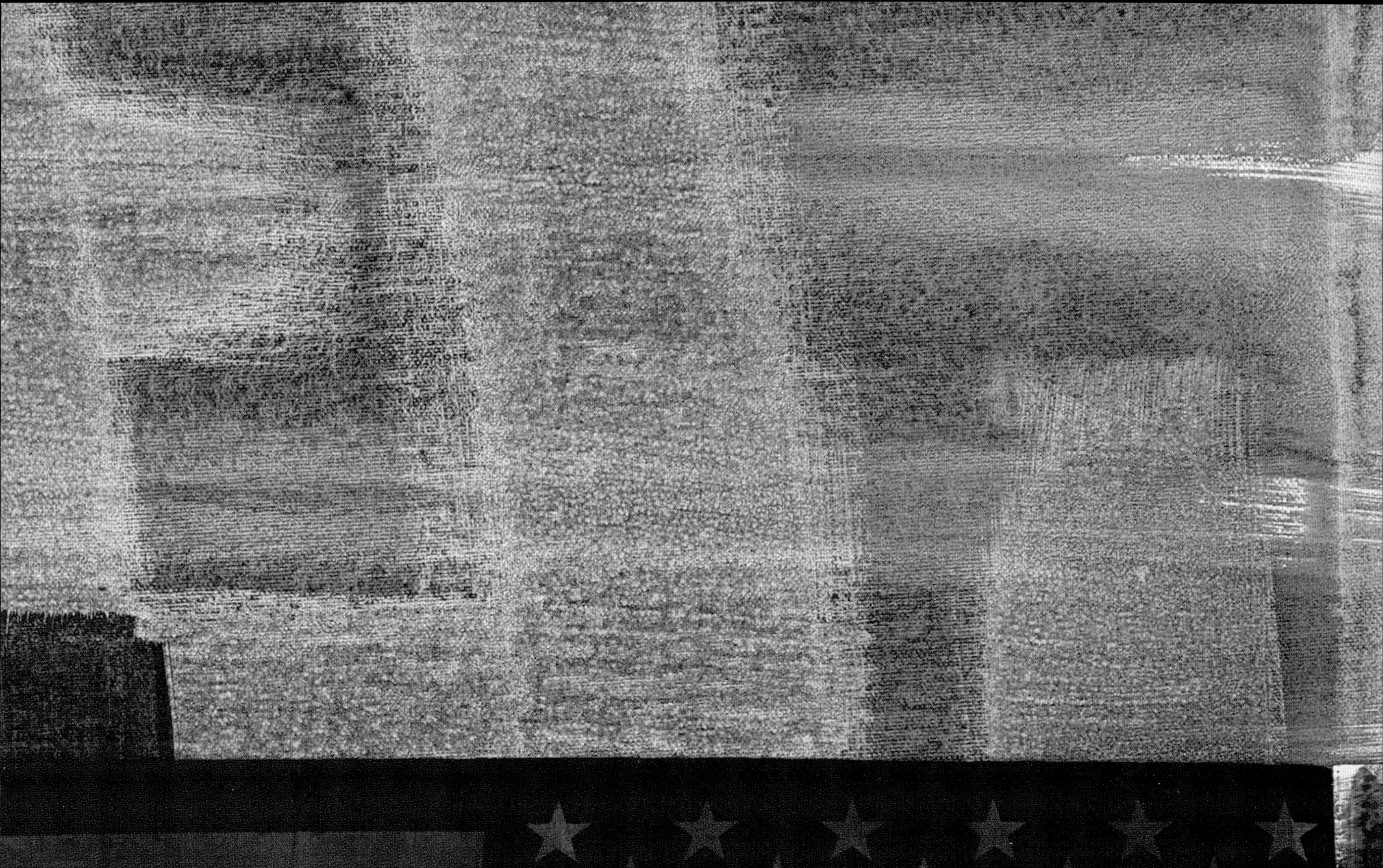

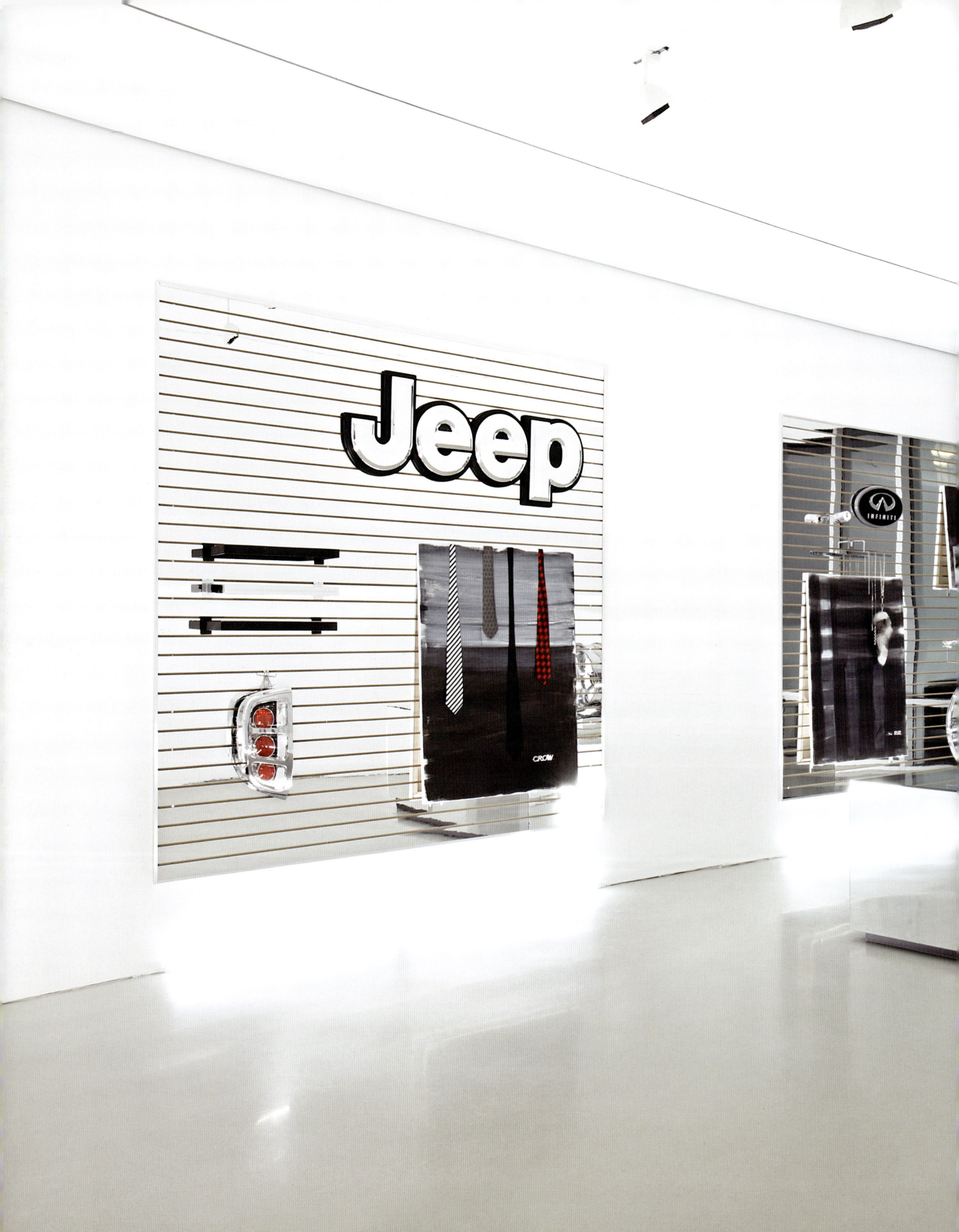

Jeep
CROW
INFINITI

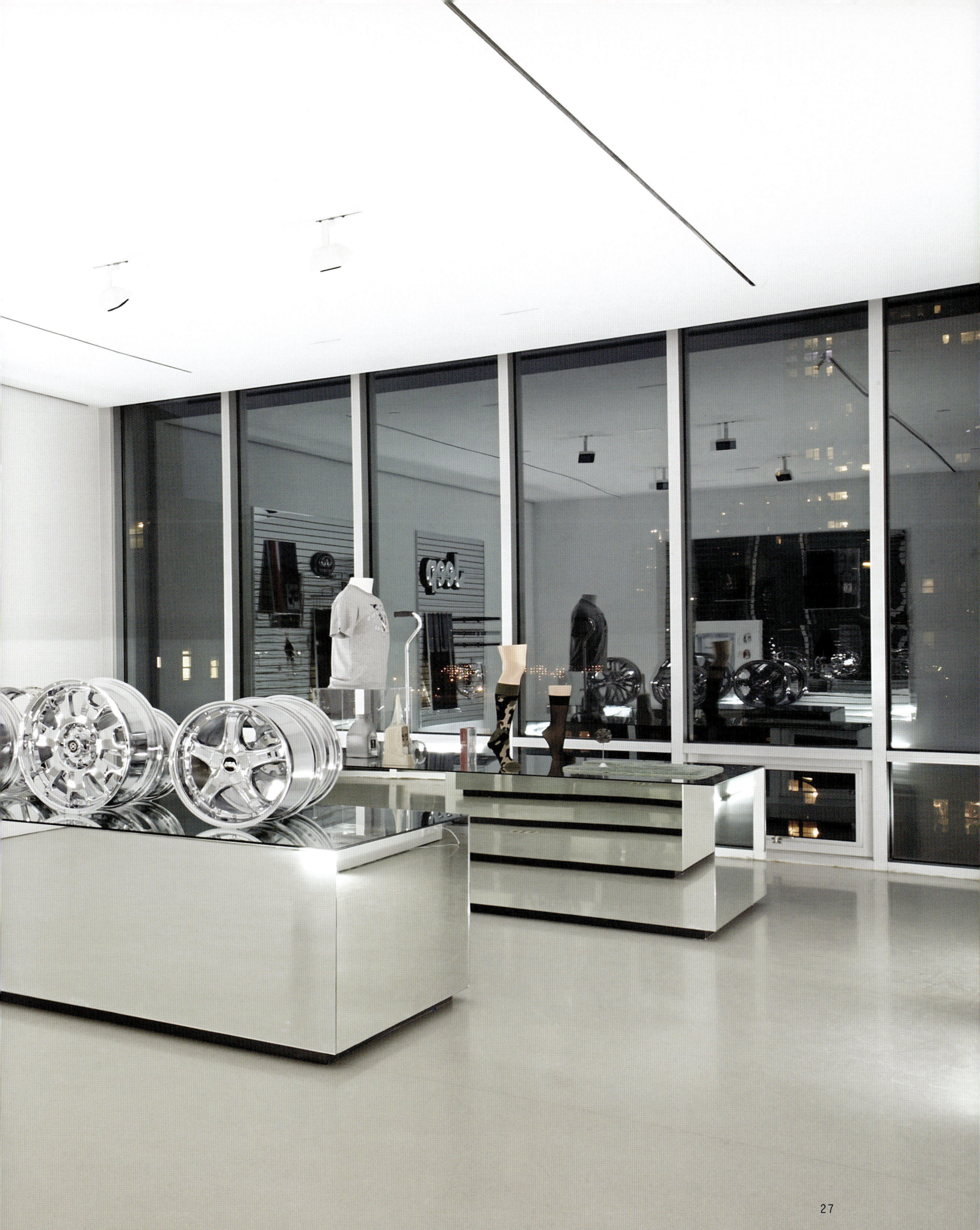

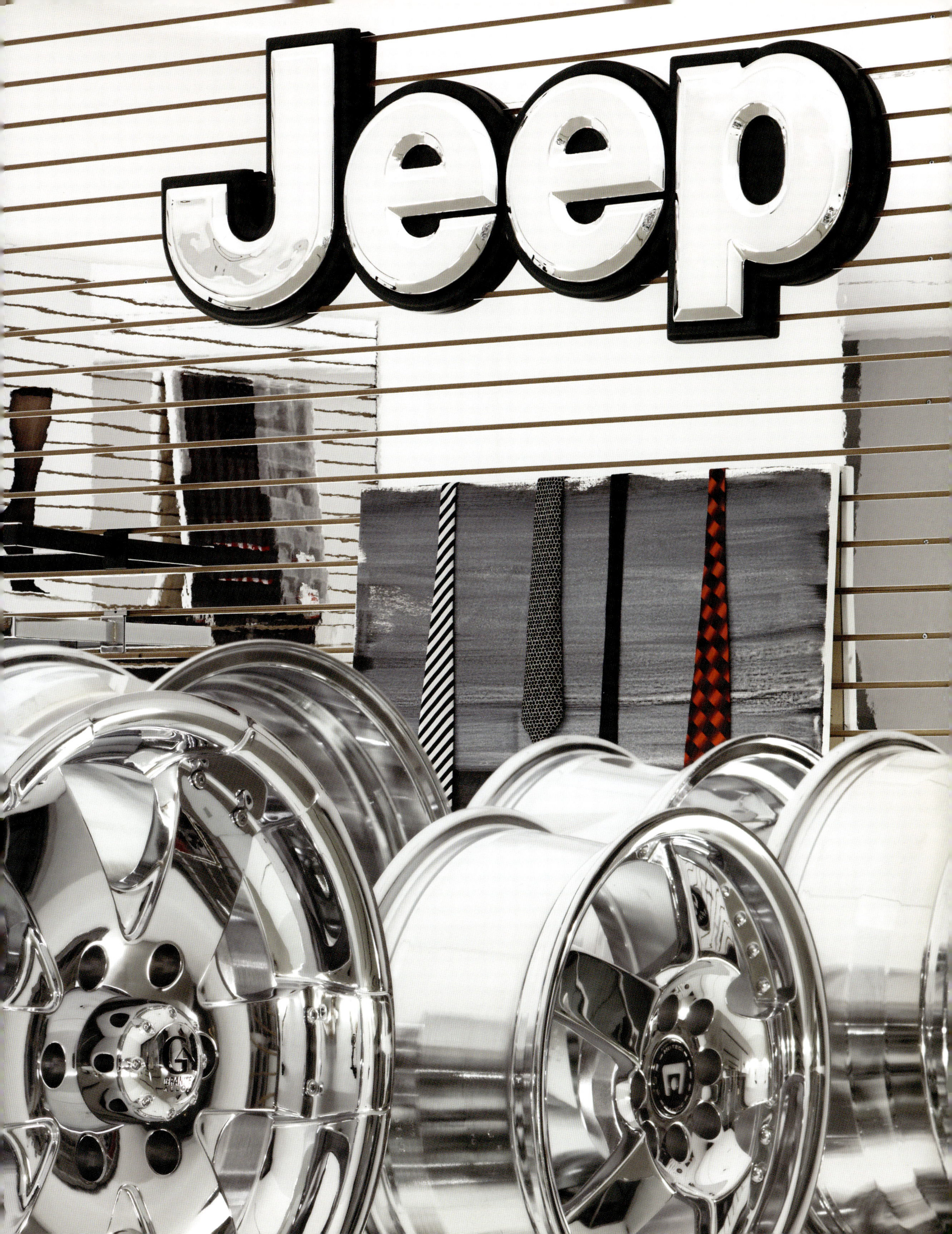

Jeep

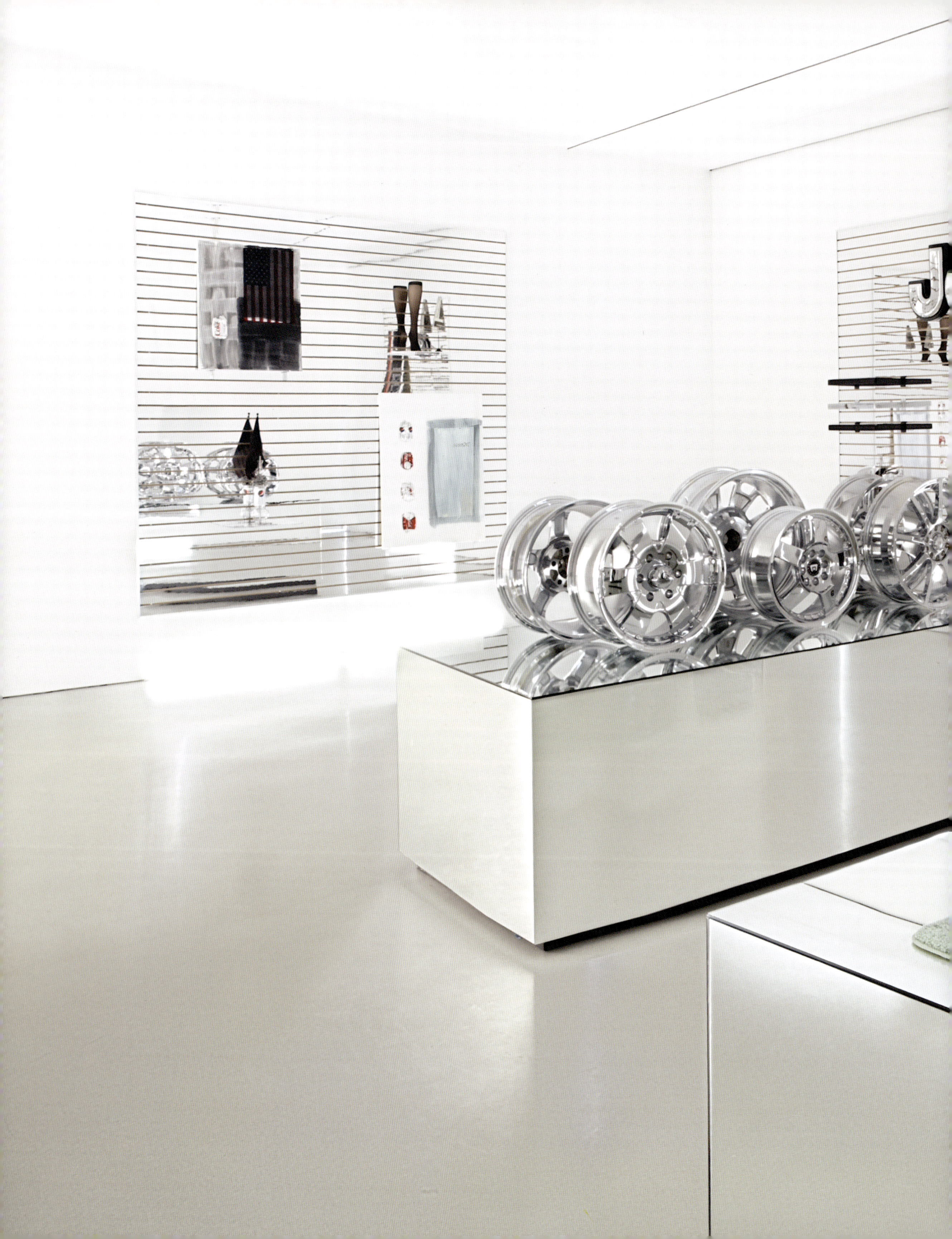

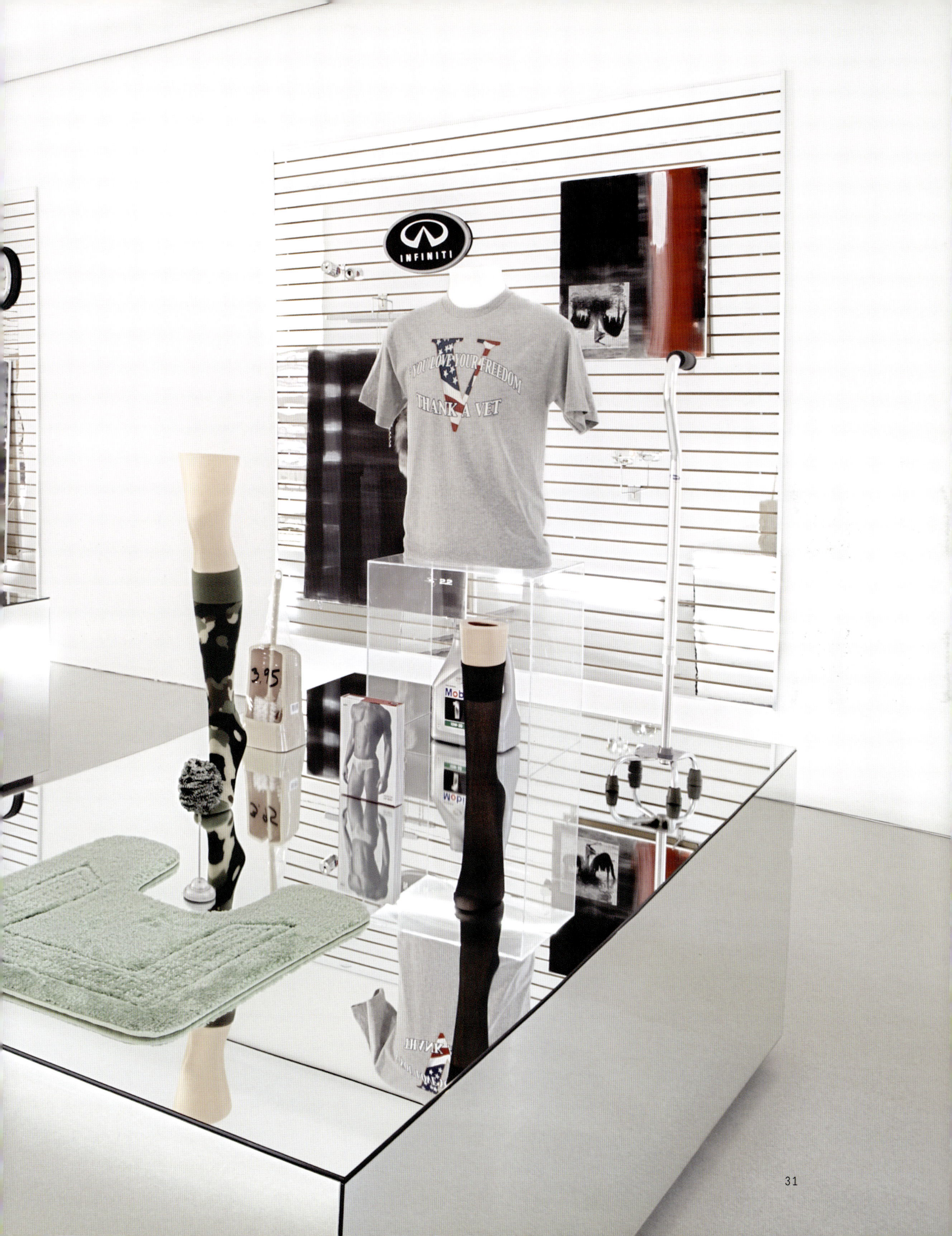

INFINITI
IF YOU LOVE YOUR FREEDOM
THANK A VET
3.95

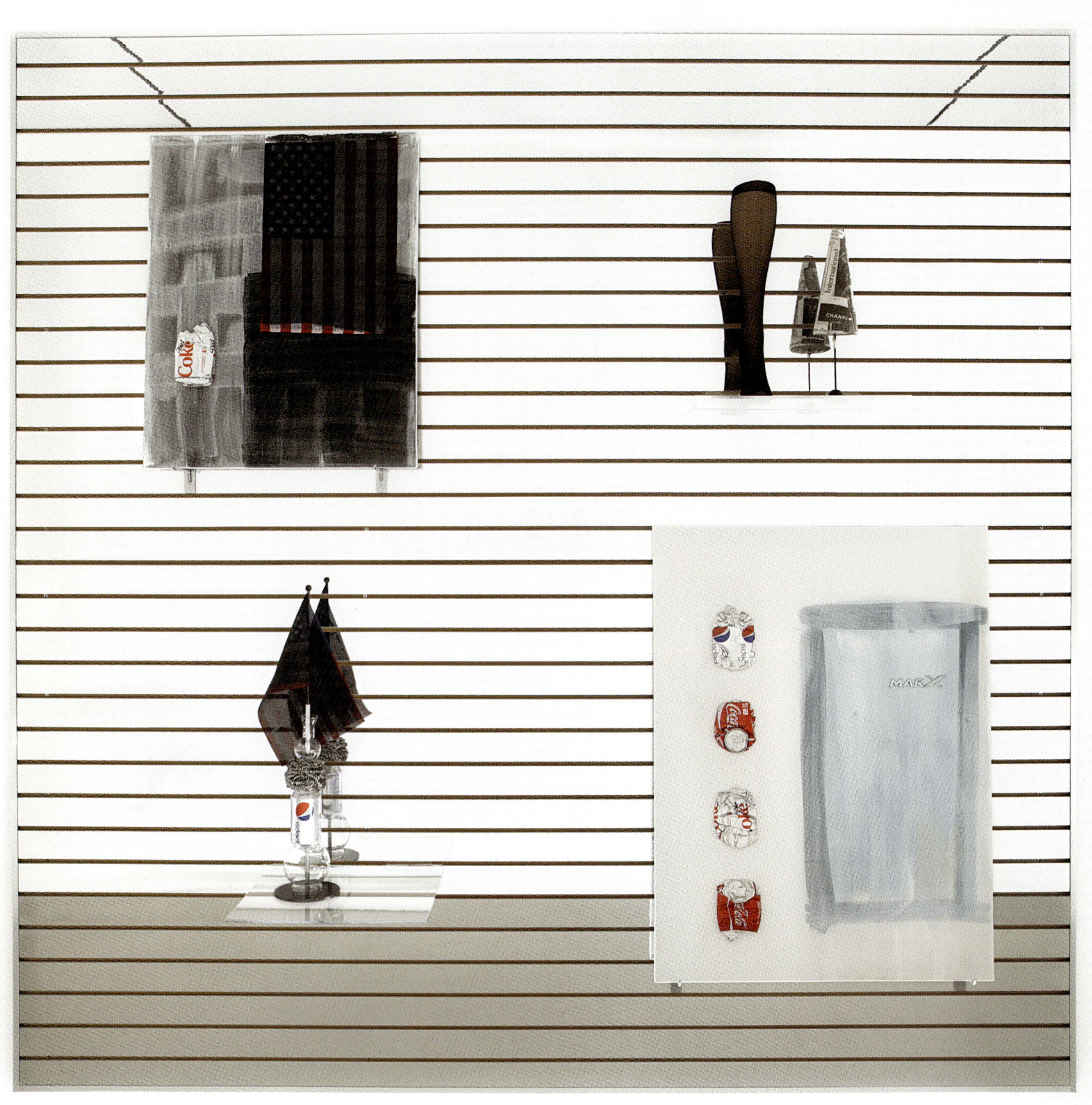

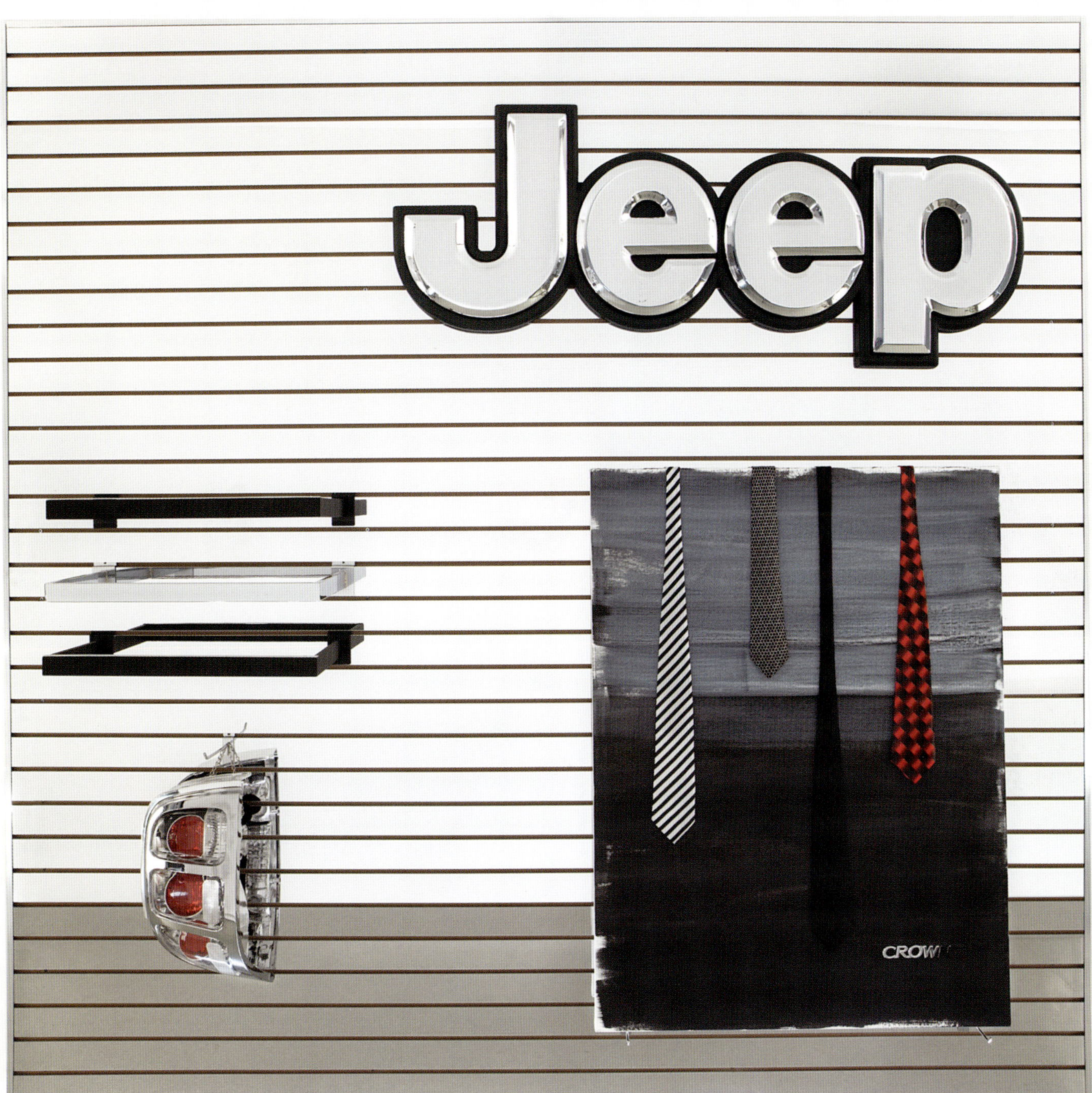
Jeep
CROWN

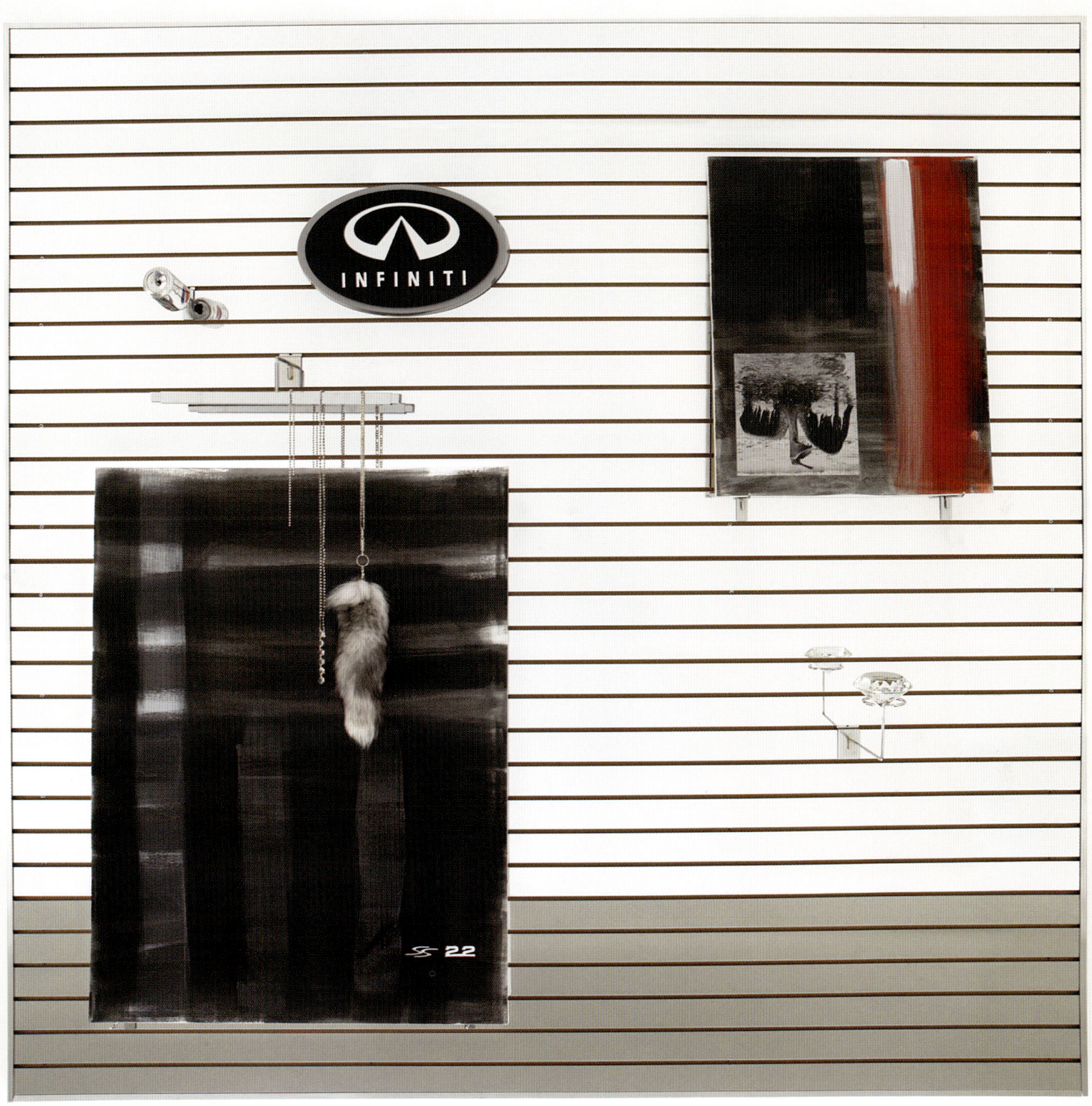

INFINITI

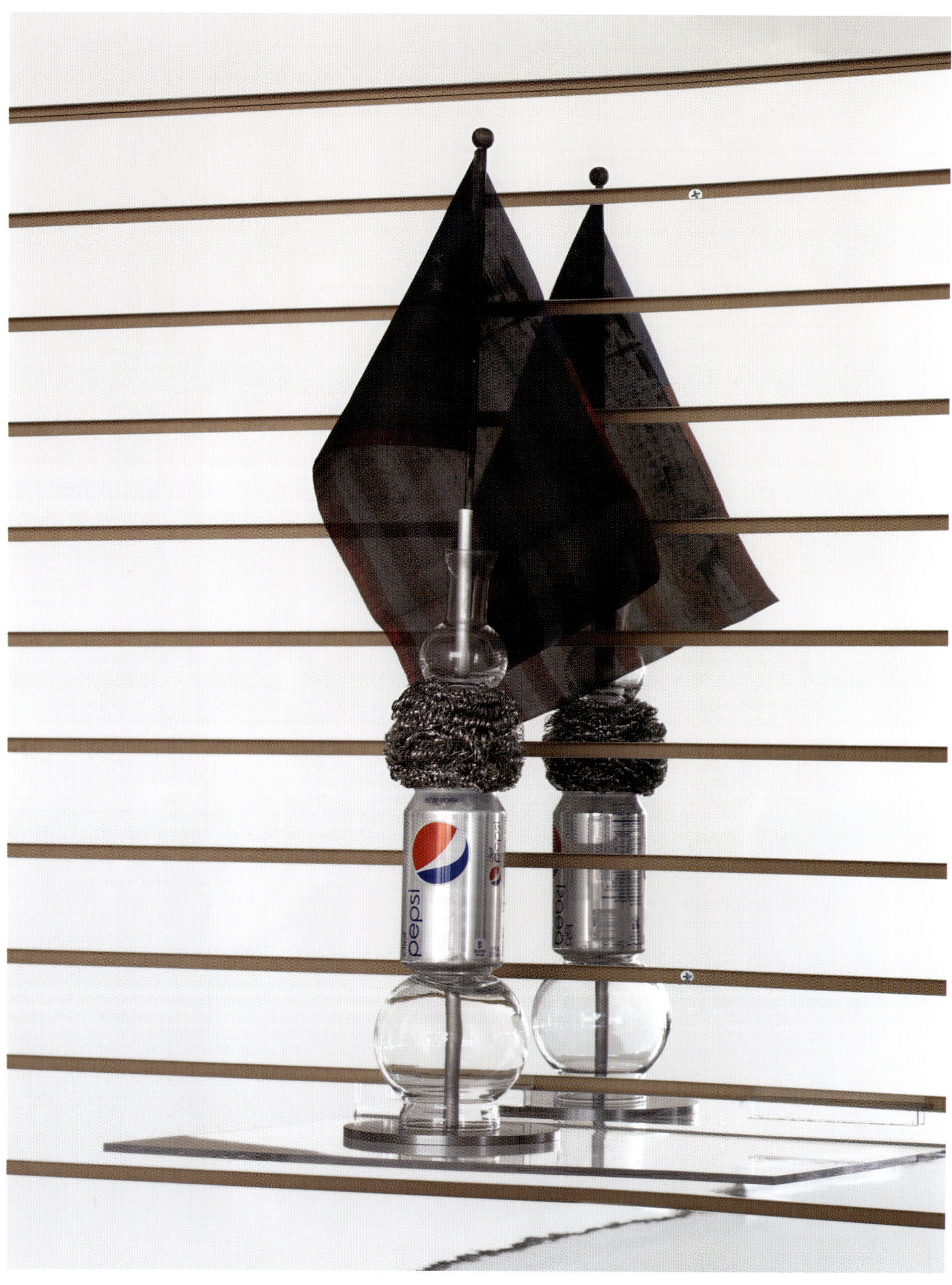

pepsi

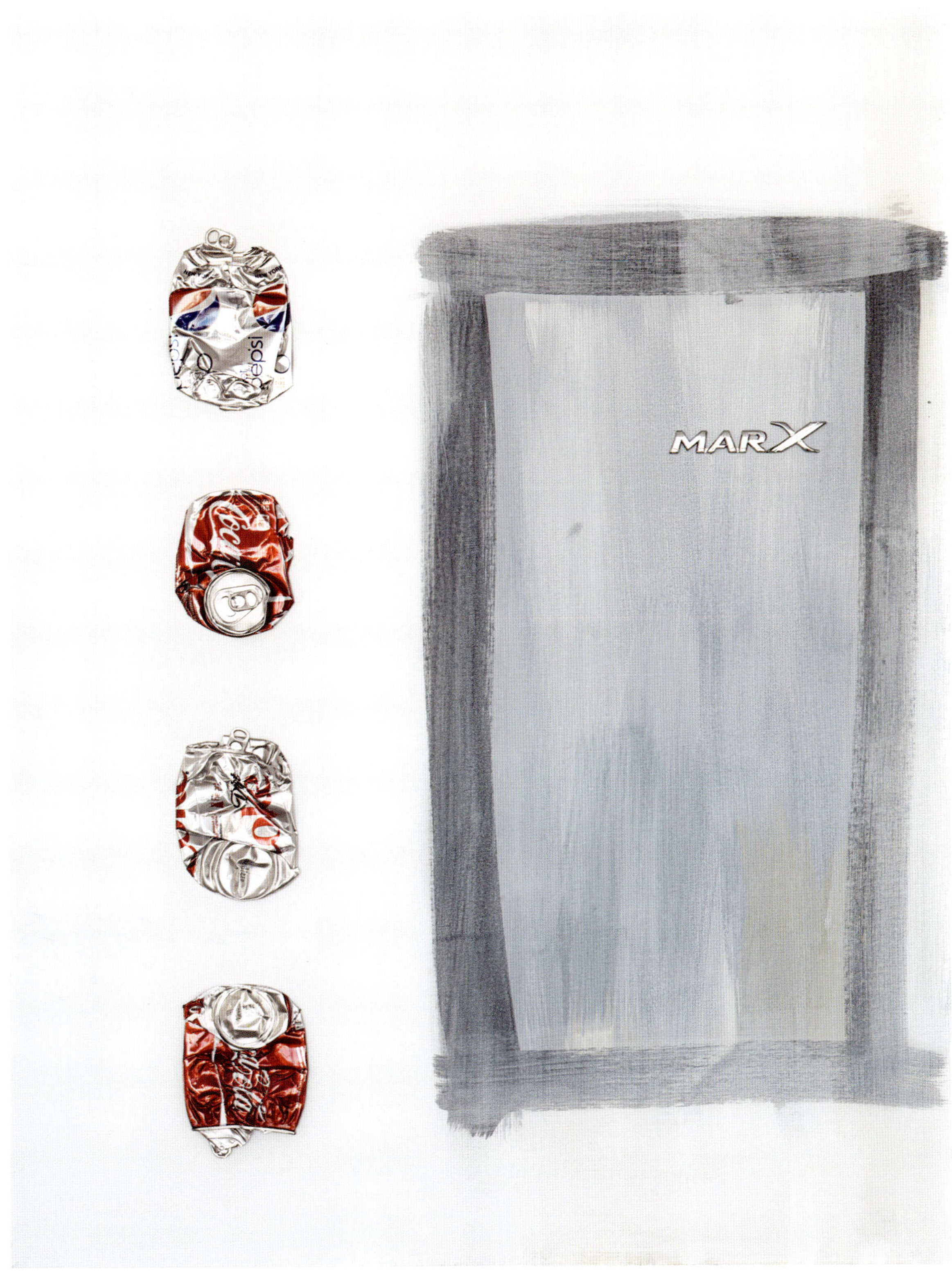

MAR X

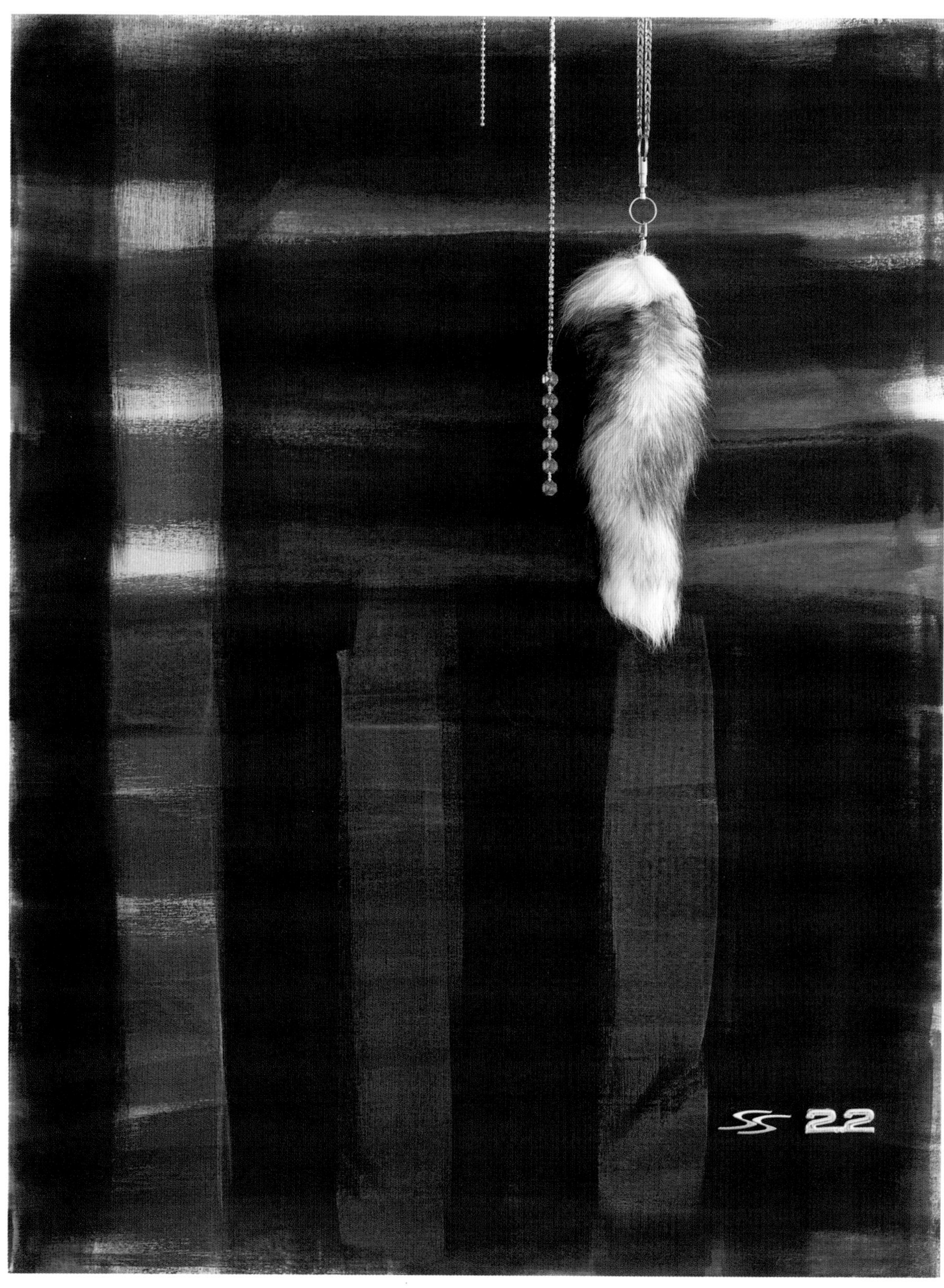

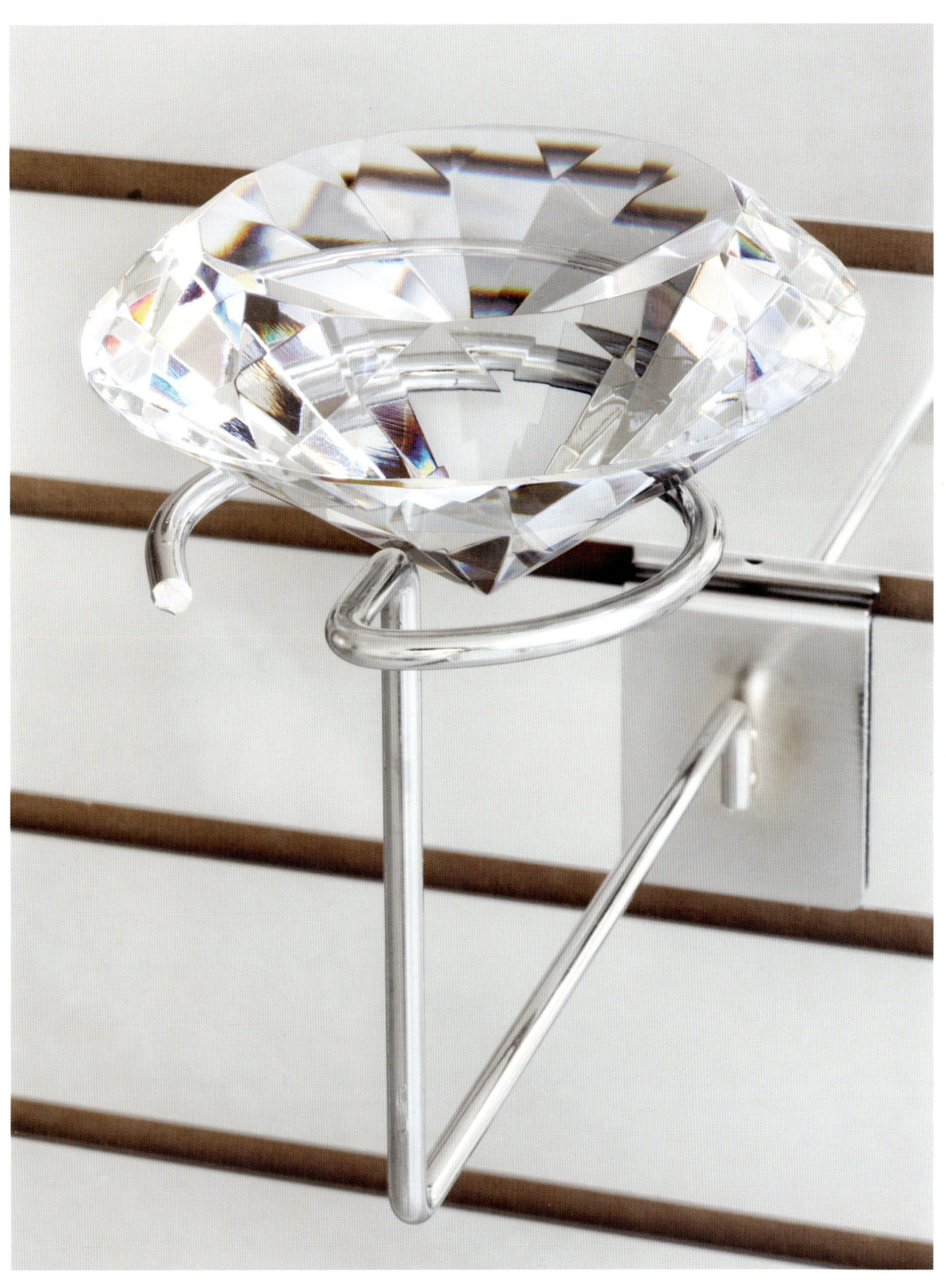

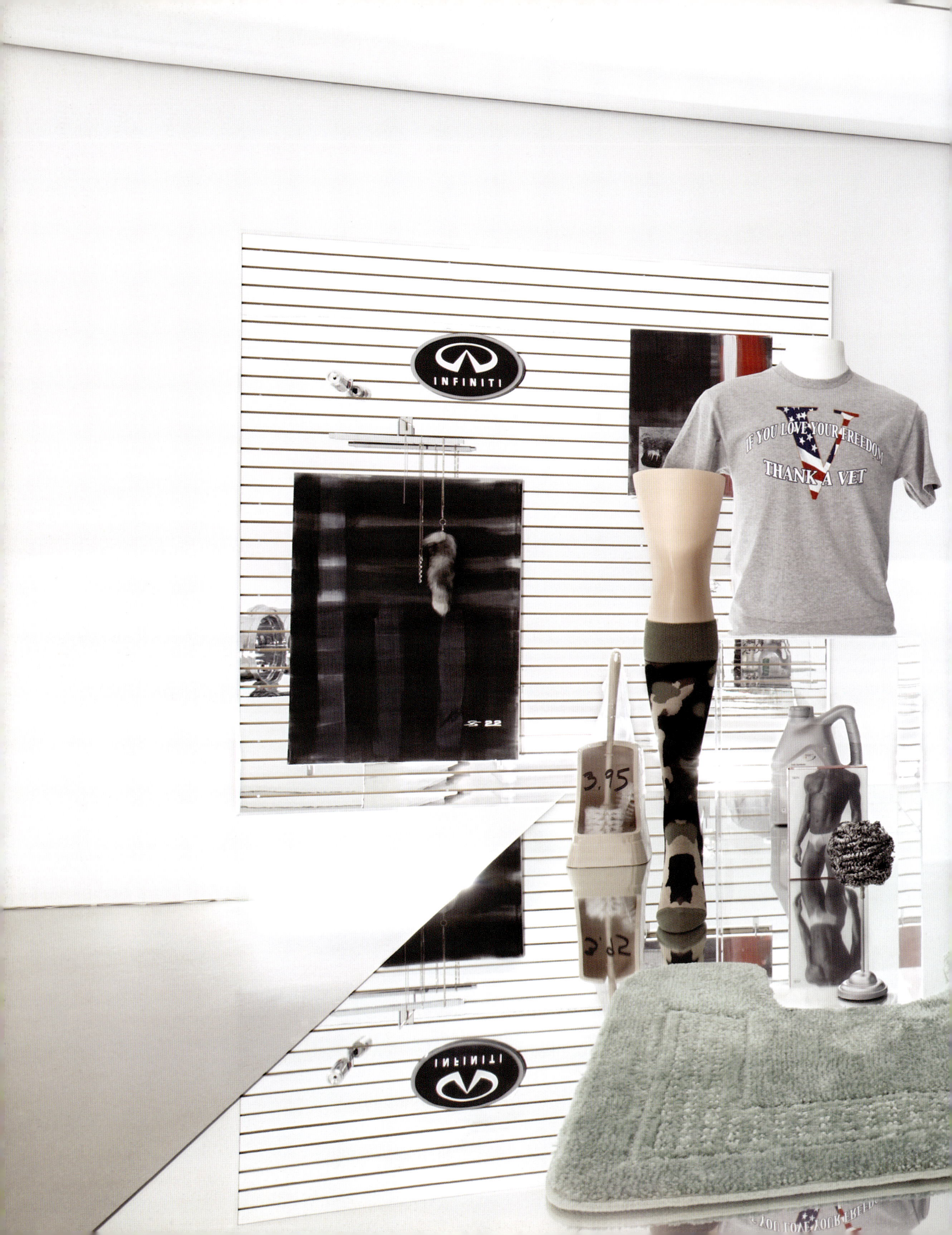
INFINITI
IF YOU LOVE YOUR FREEDOM
THANK A VET
3.95

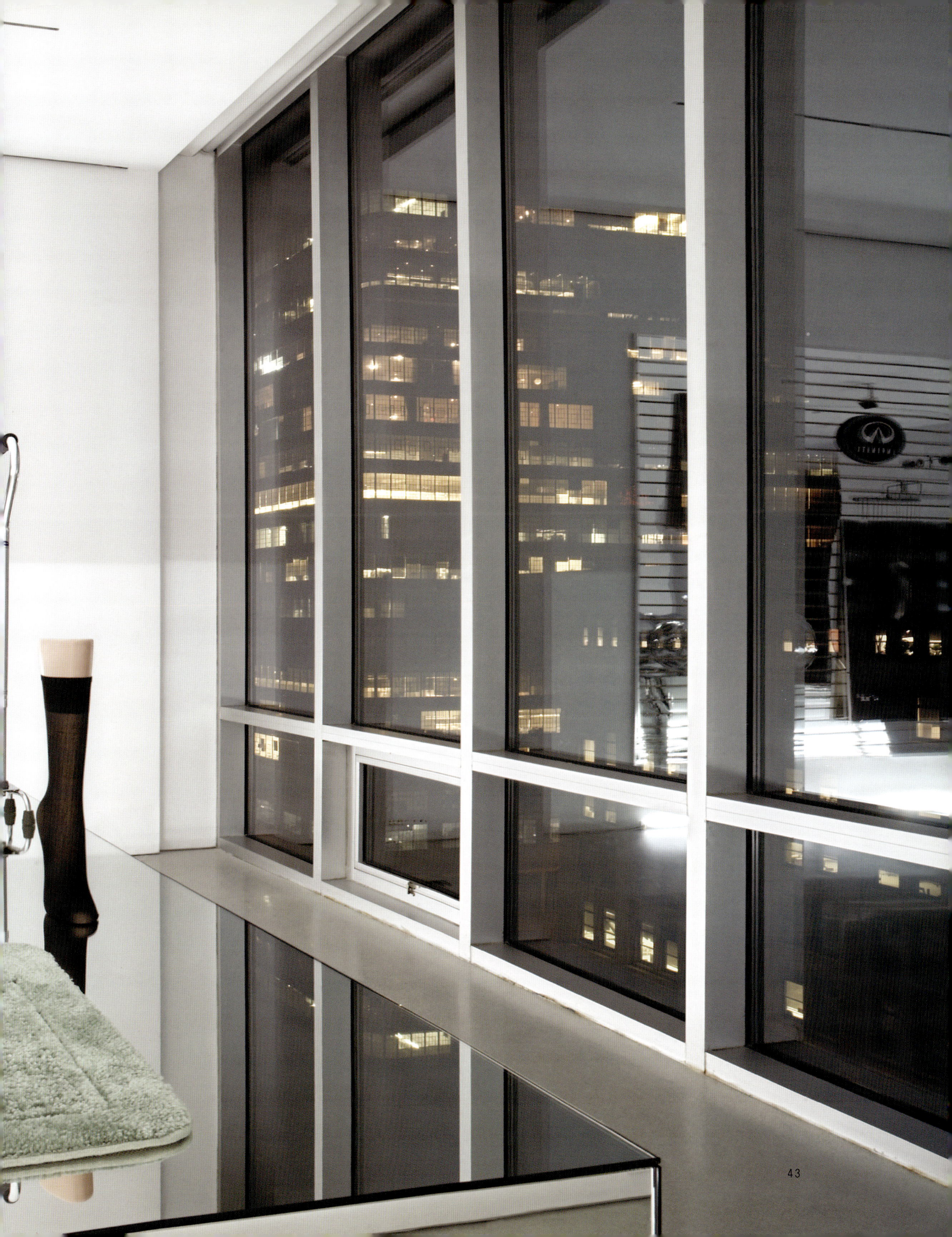

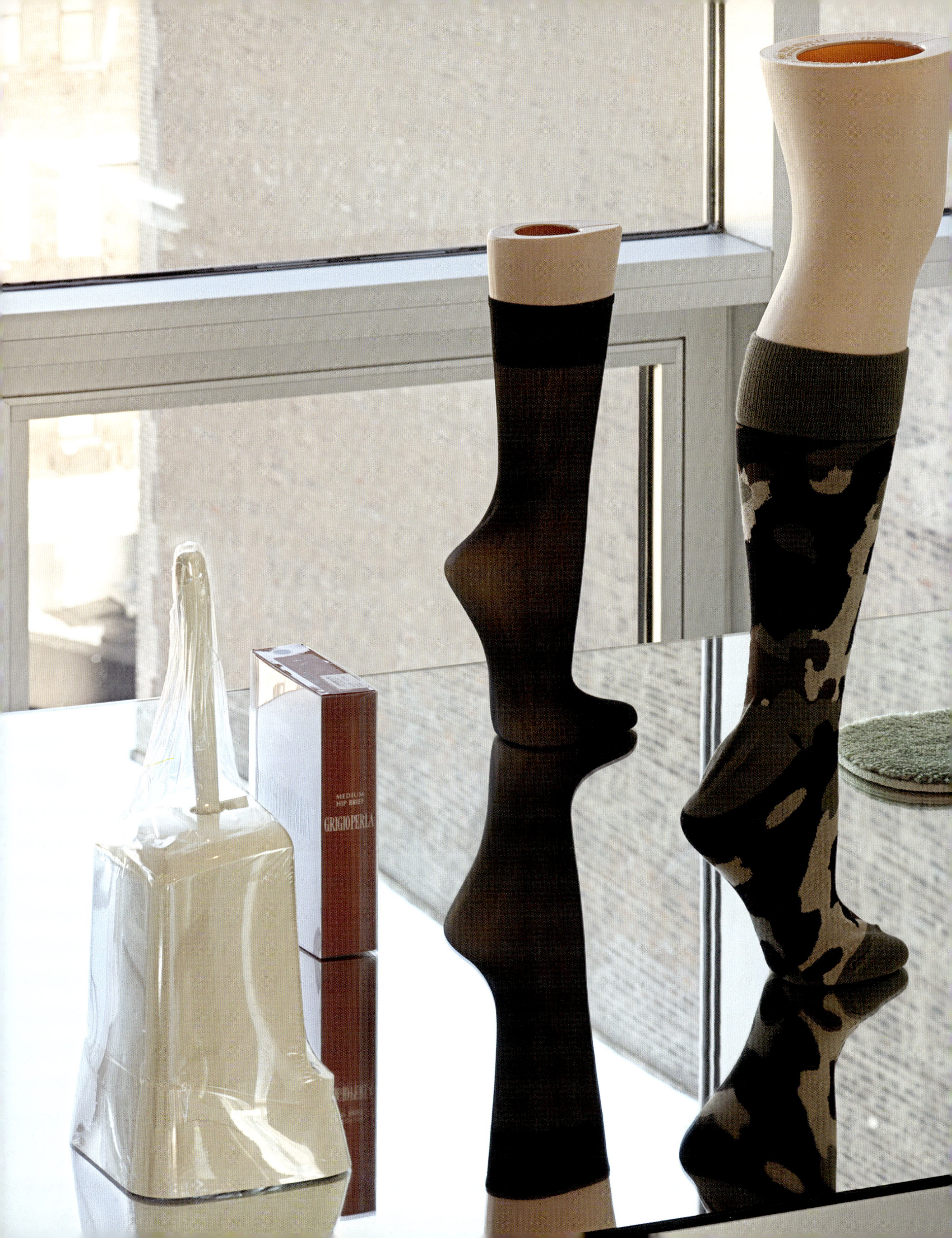
MEDIUM
HIP BRIEF
GRIGIOPERLA

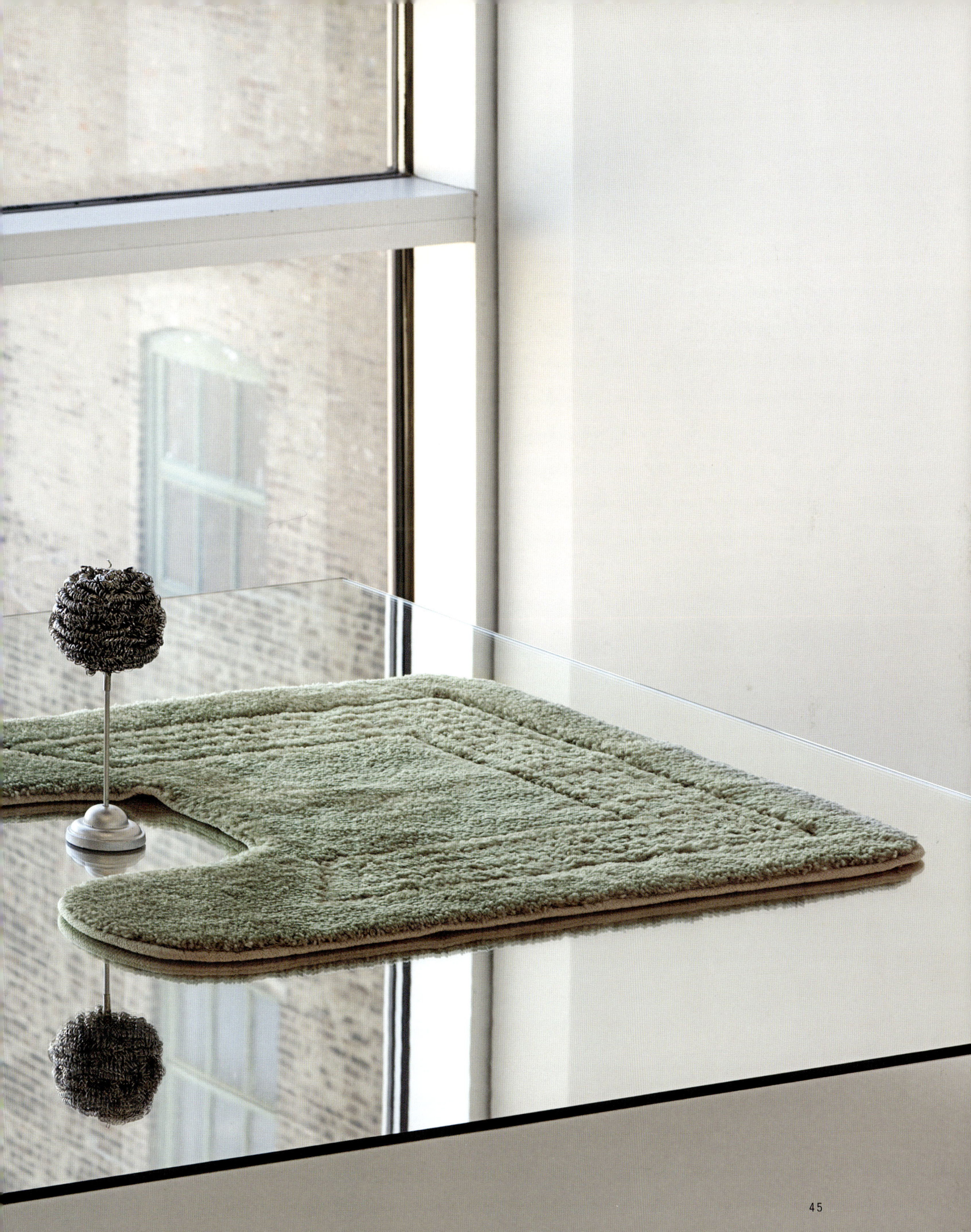

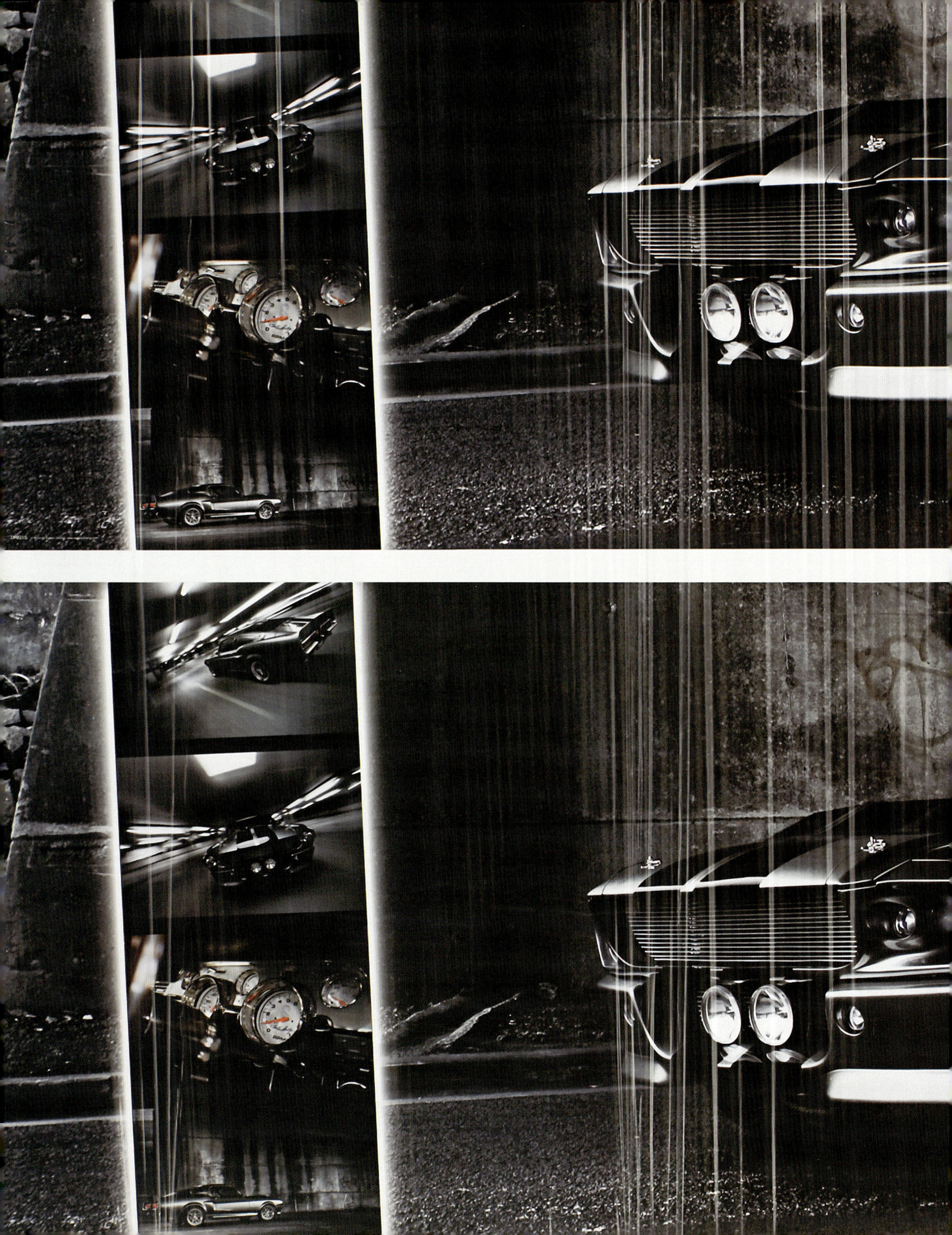

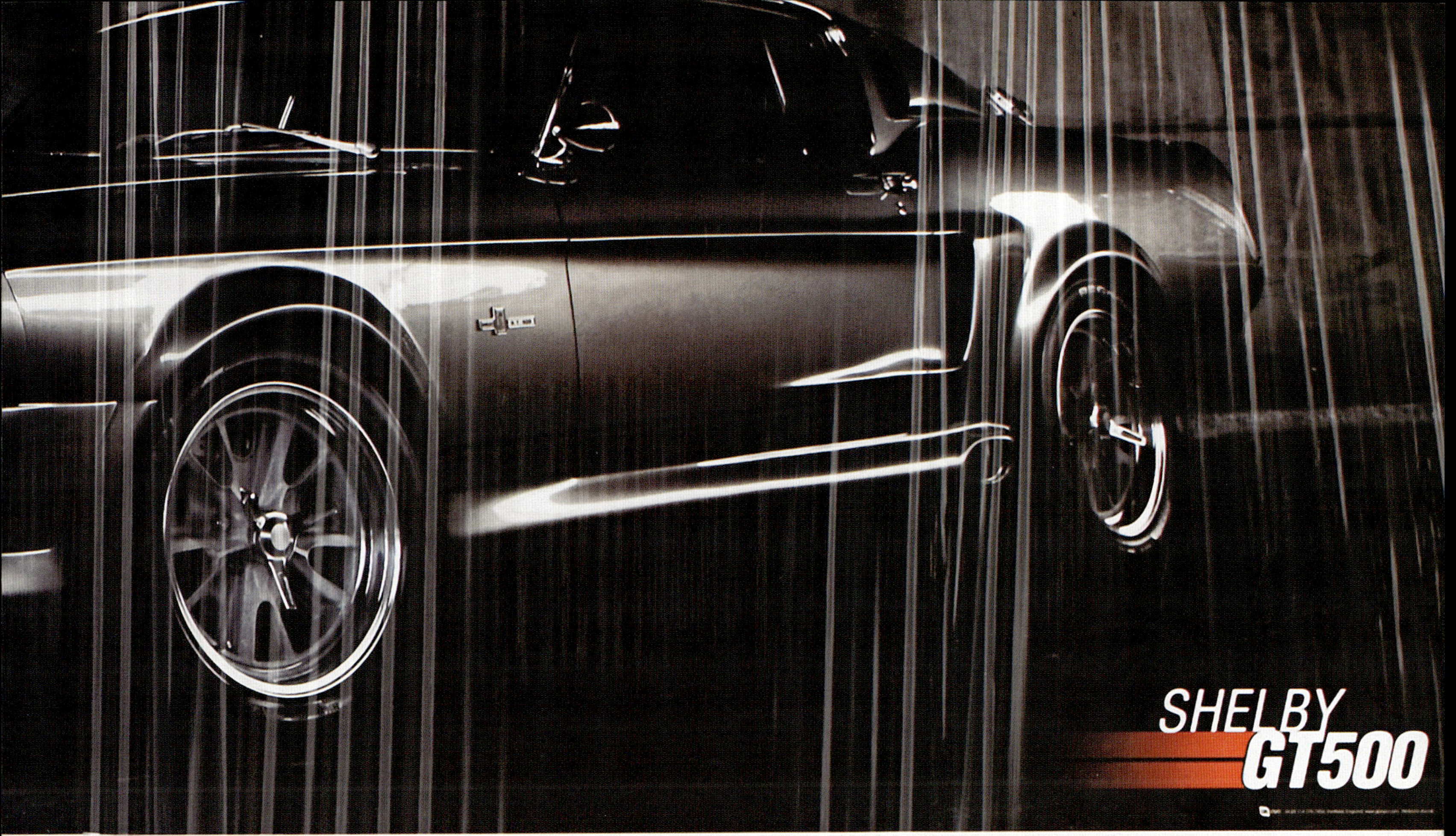

SHELBY
GT500

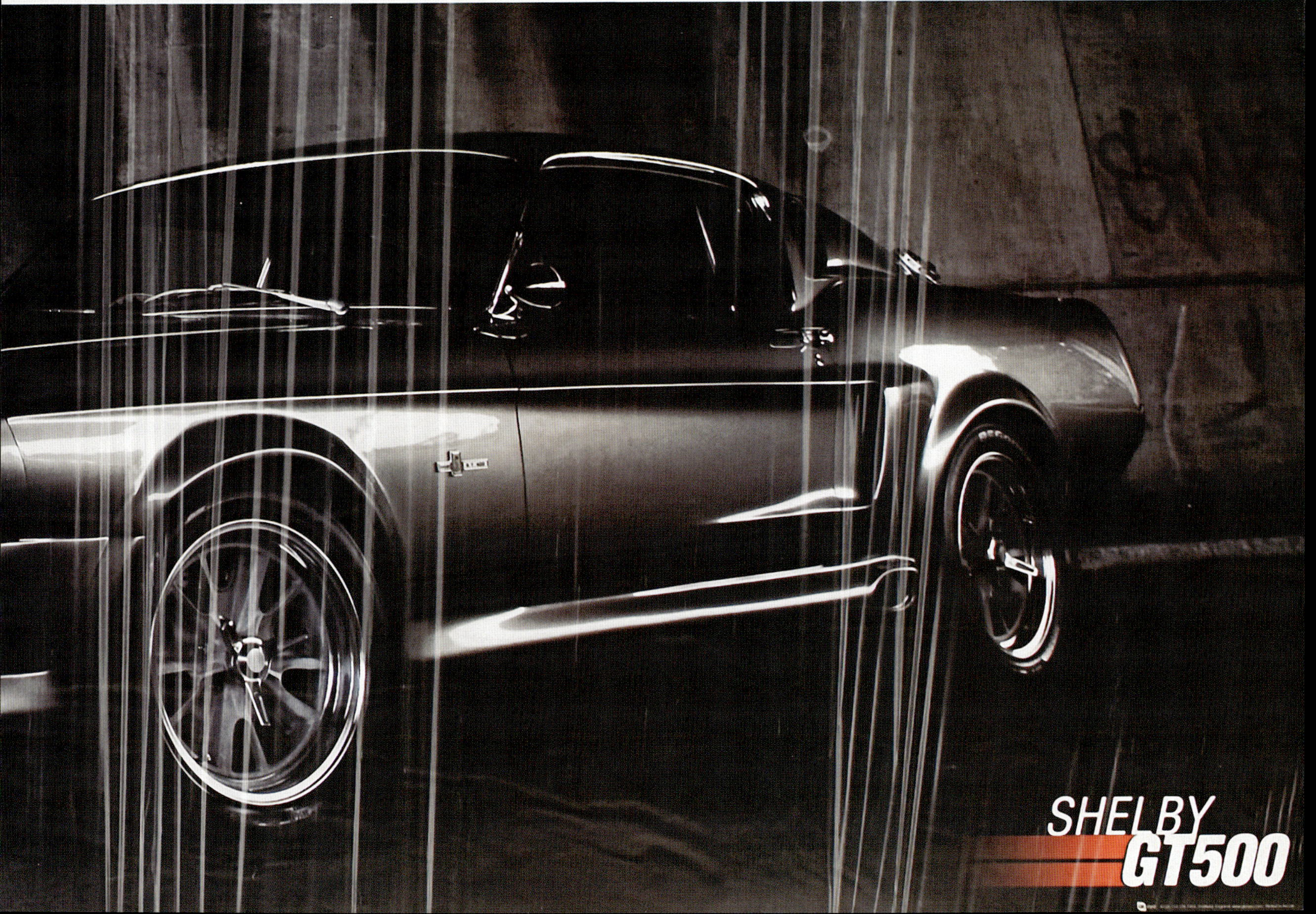

SHELBY
GT500

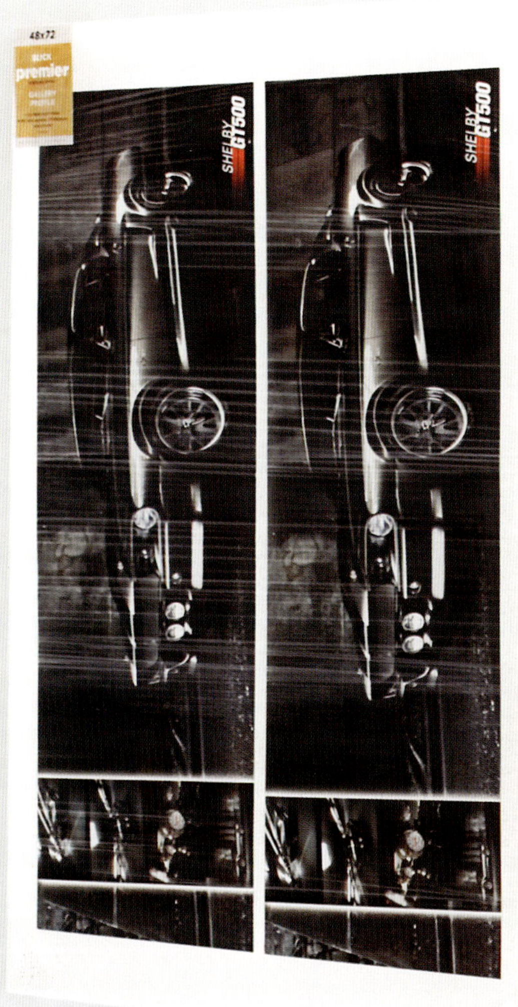

48x72
BLICK premier
GALLERY PROFILE
SHELBY GT500
SHELBY GT500

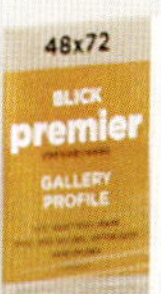

48x72
BLICK premier
GALLERY PROFILE

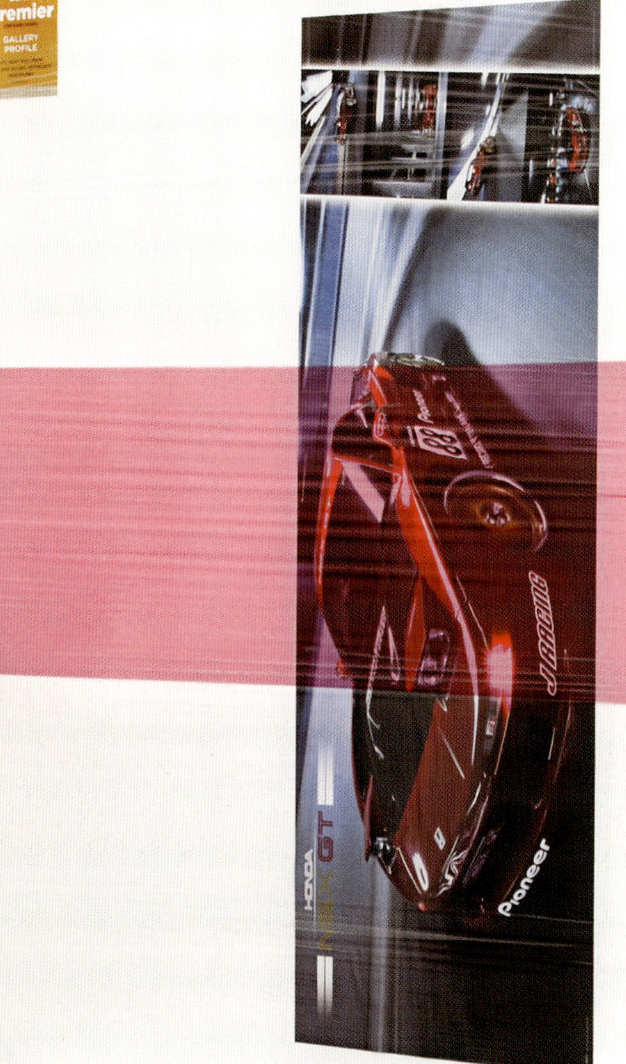

HONDA NSX GT
Pioneer
J RACING
Pioneer

Stretched
cANVAS
¾" solid wood frame
36 x 48
THE
aRT
STORE

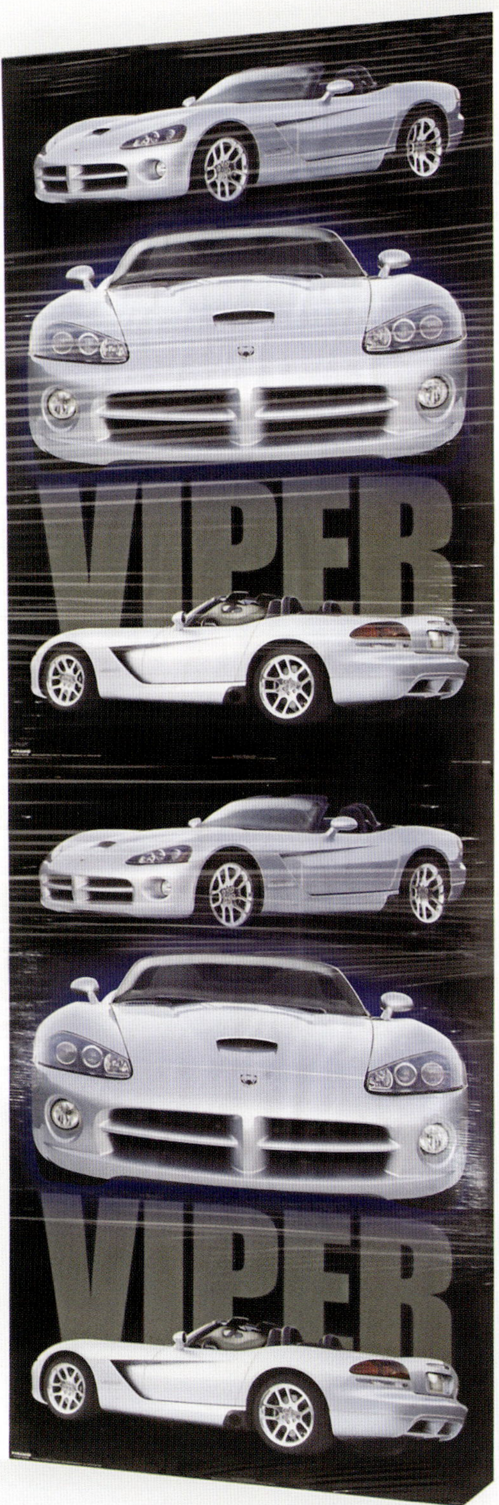

VIPER
VIPER

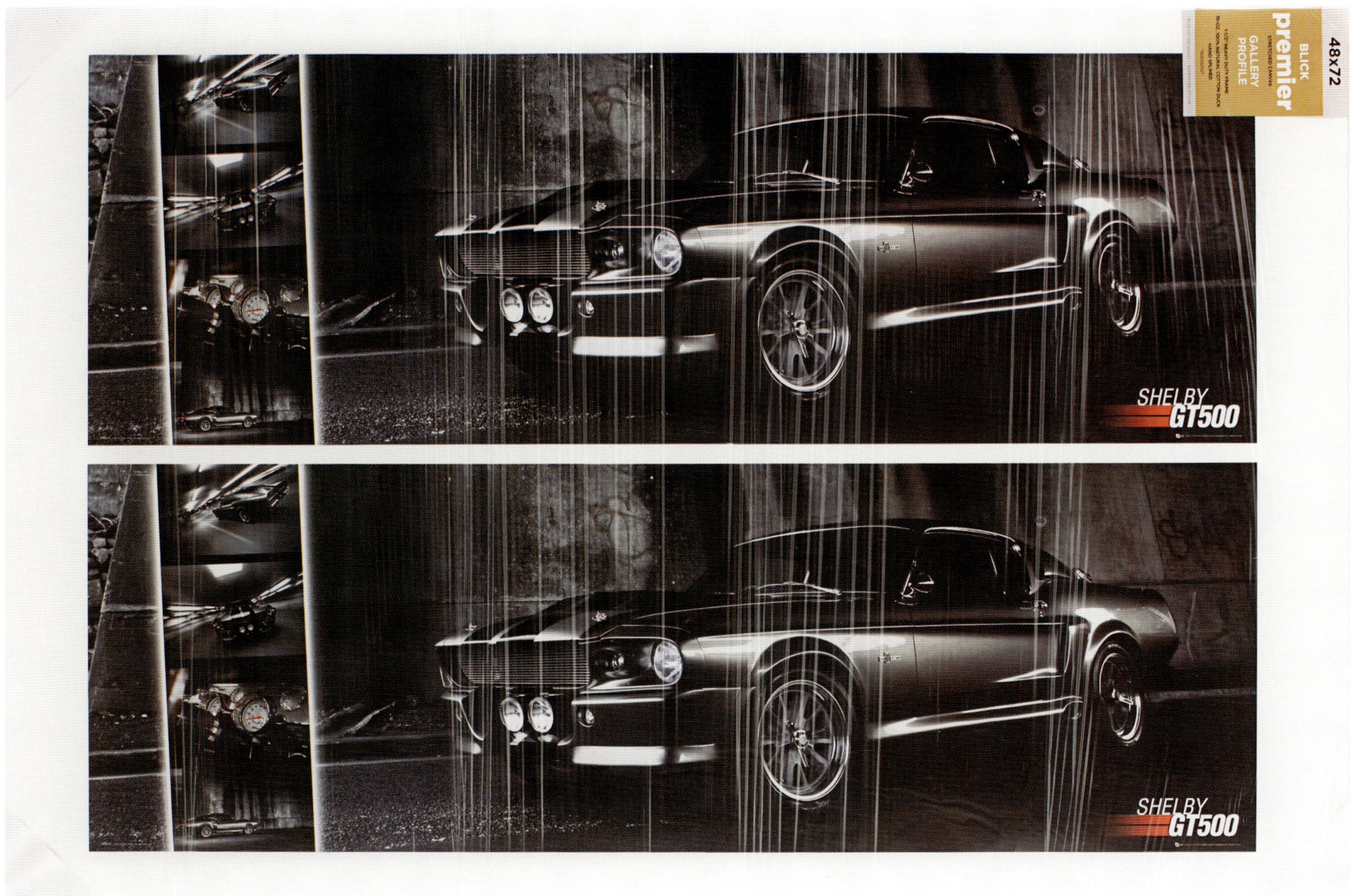
48x72
BLICK
premier
STRETCHED CANVAS
GALLERY
PROFILE
1-1/2" HEAVY DUTY FRAME
10-OZ. 100% NATURAL COTTON DUCK
HAND SPLINED
SHELBY
GT500
SHELBY
GT500

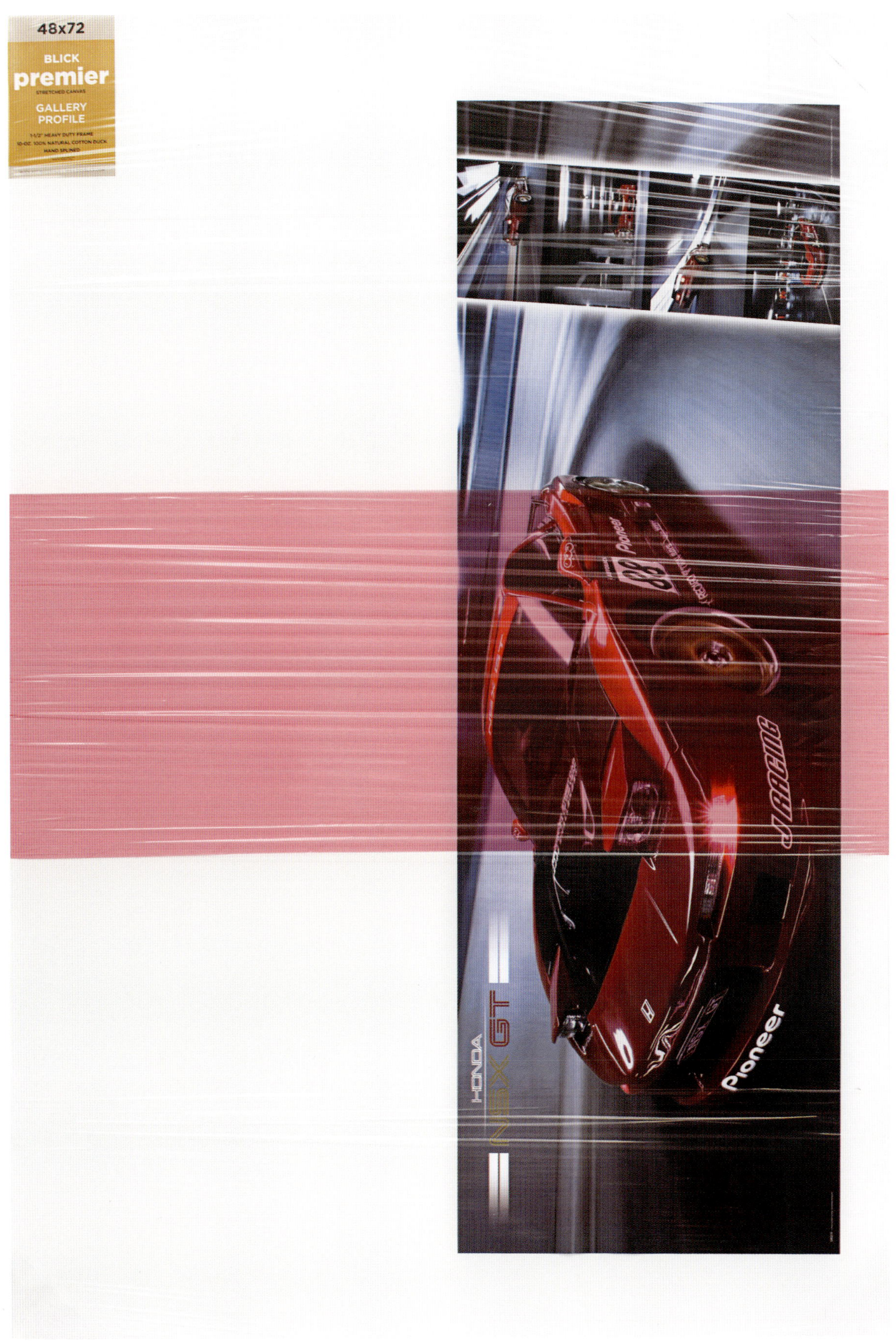
HONDA
NSX GT
J.RACING
Pioneer
Pioneer

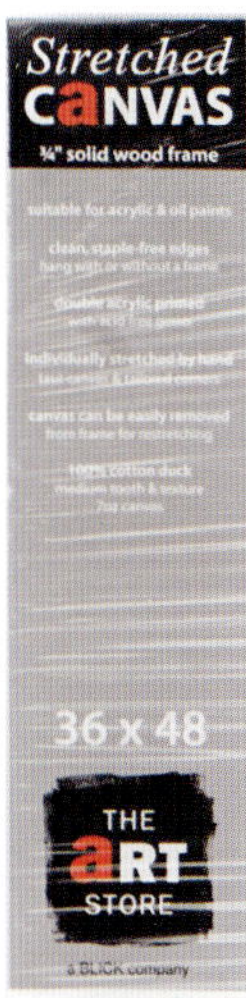

Stretched
CANVAS
¾" solid wood frame
36 x 48
THE
aRT
STORE

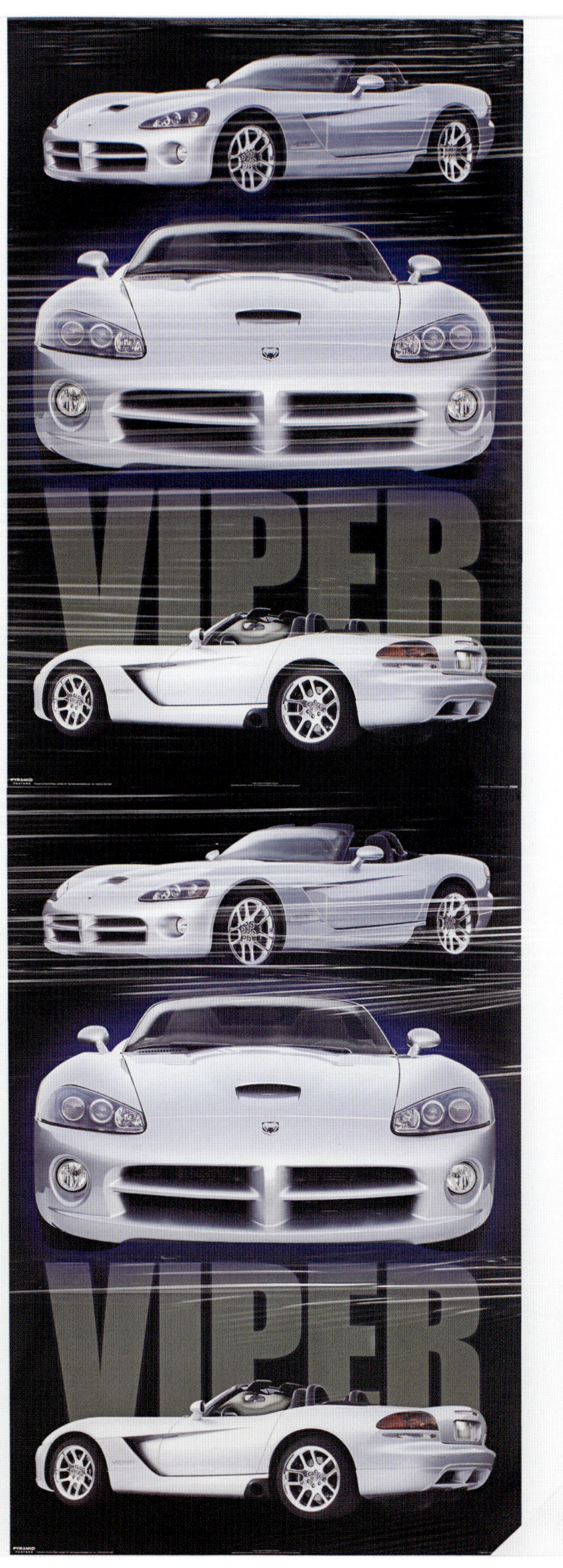

VIPER
VIPER

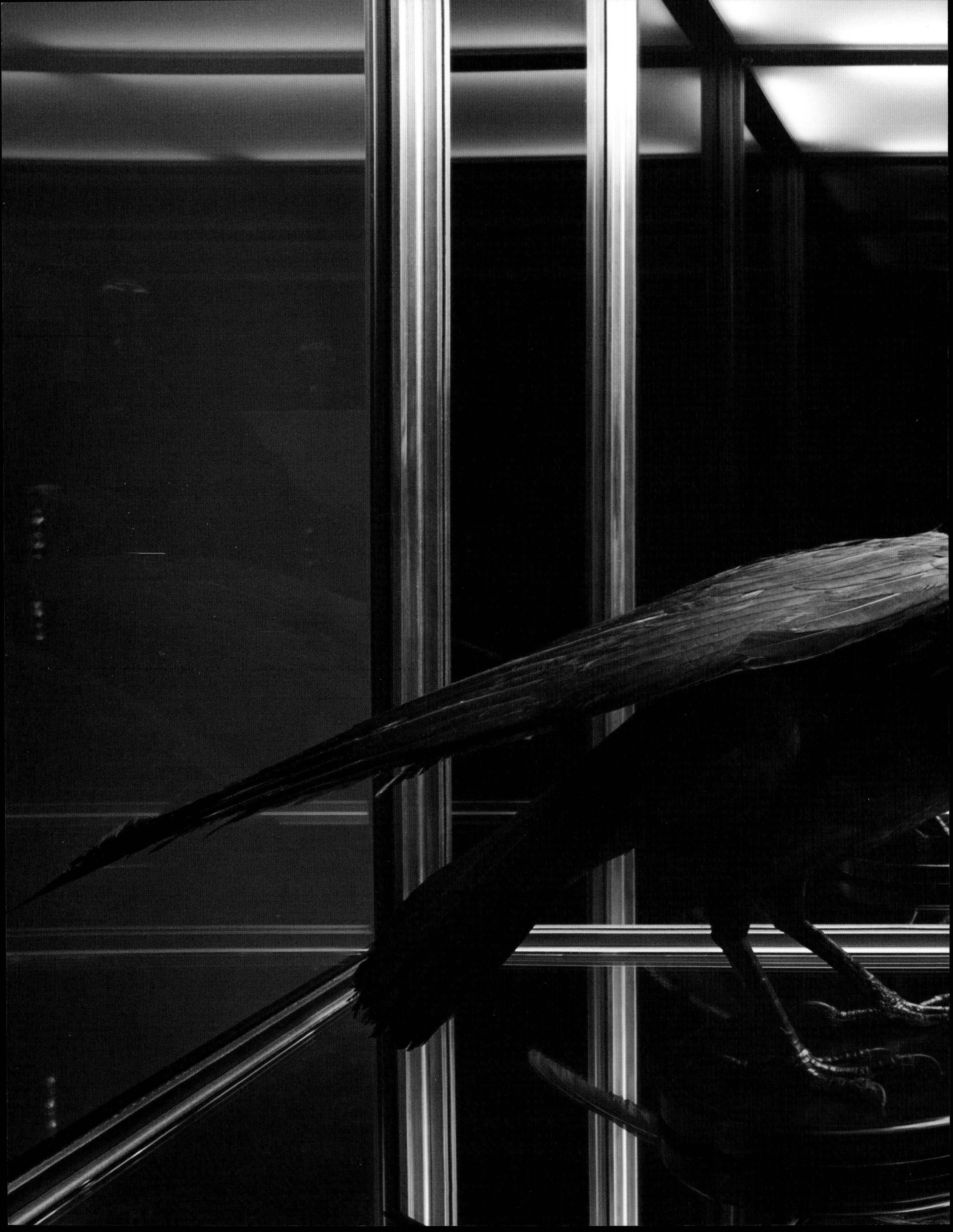

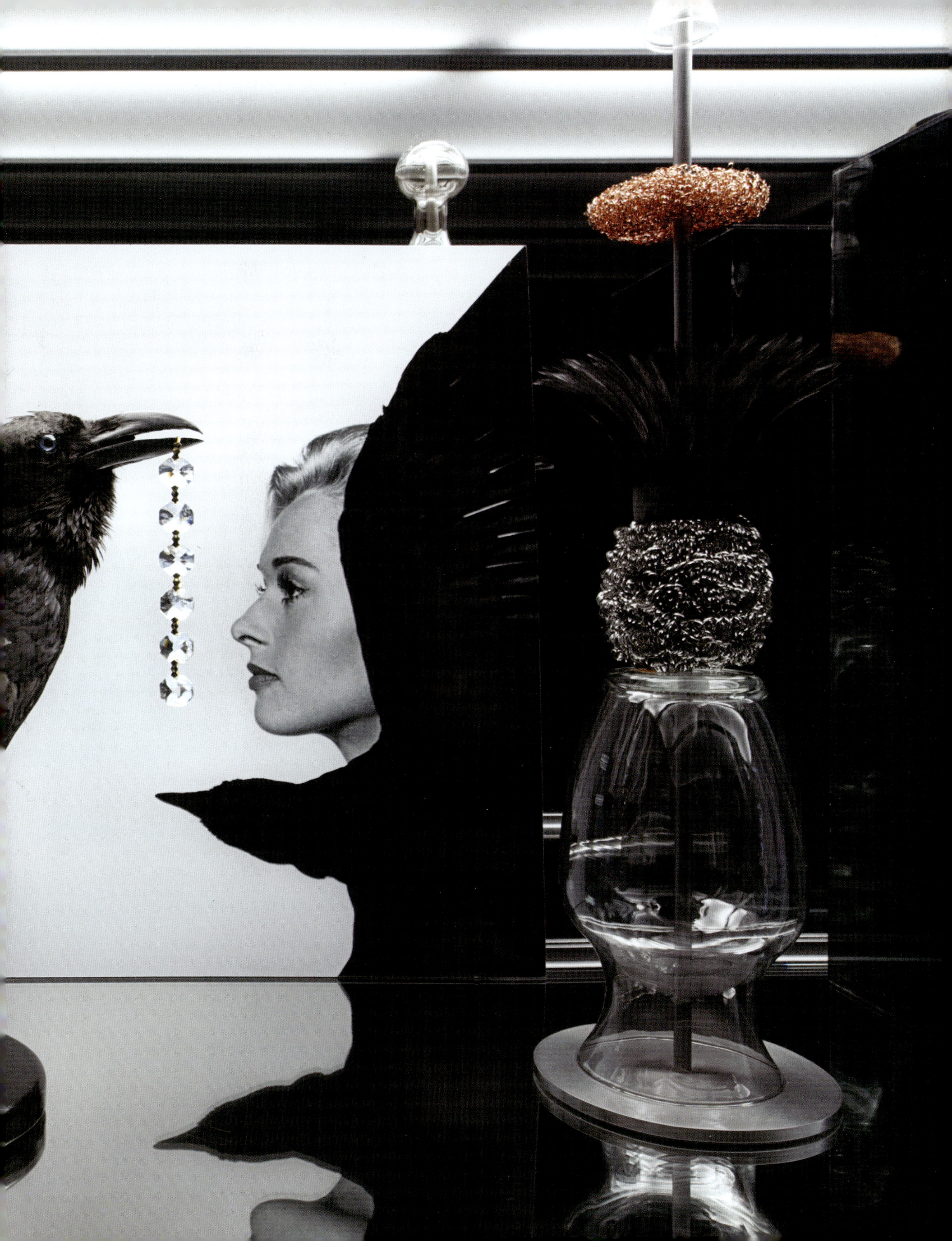

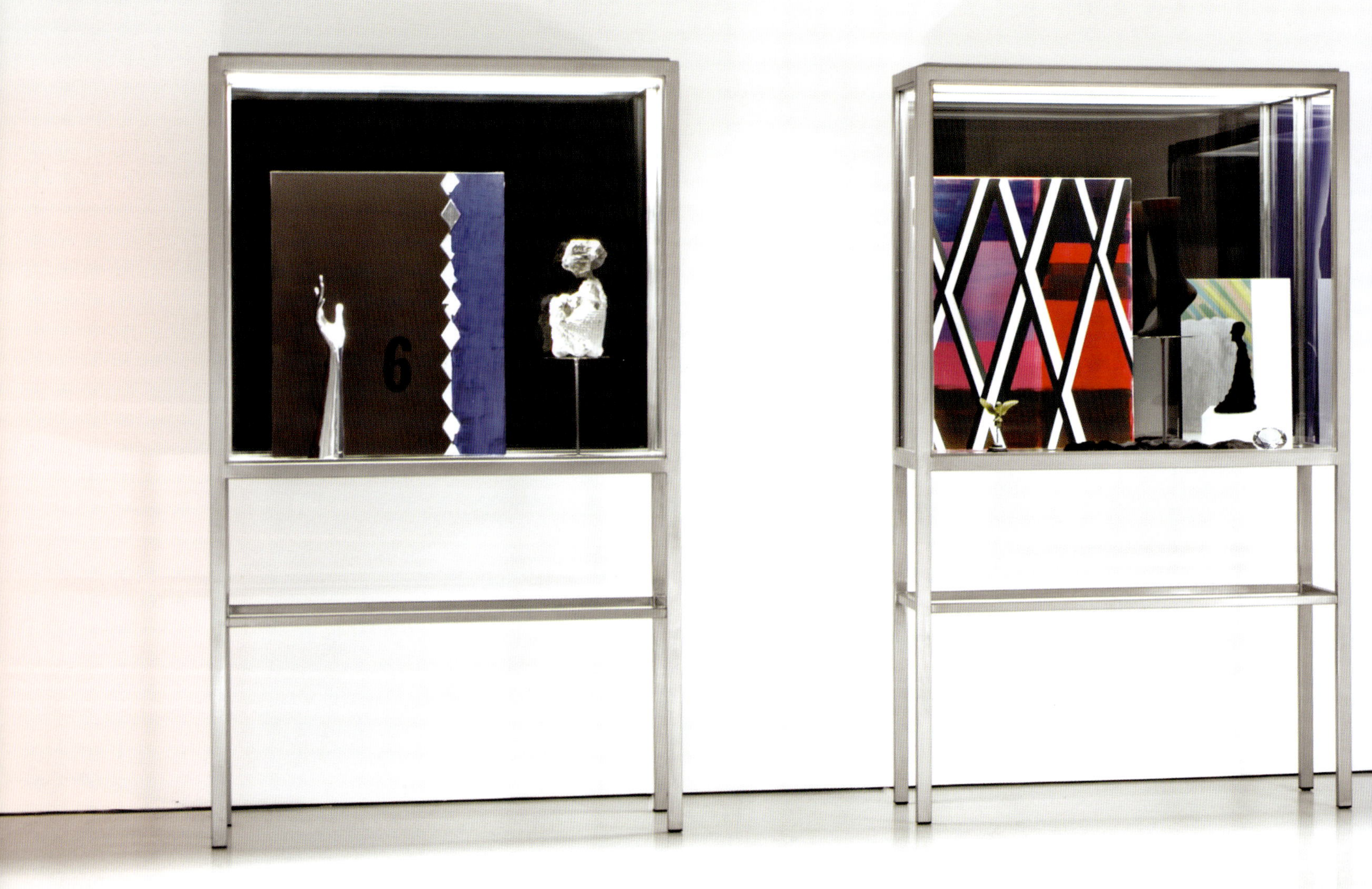

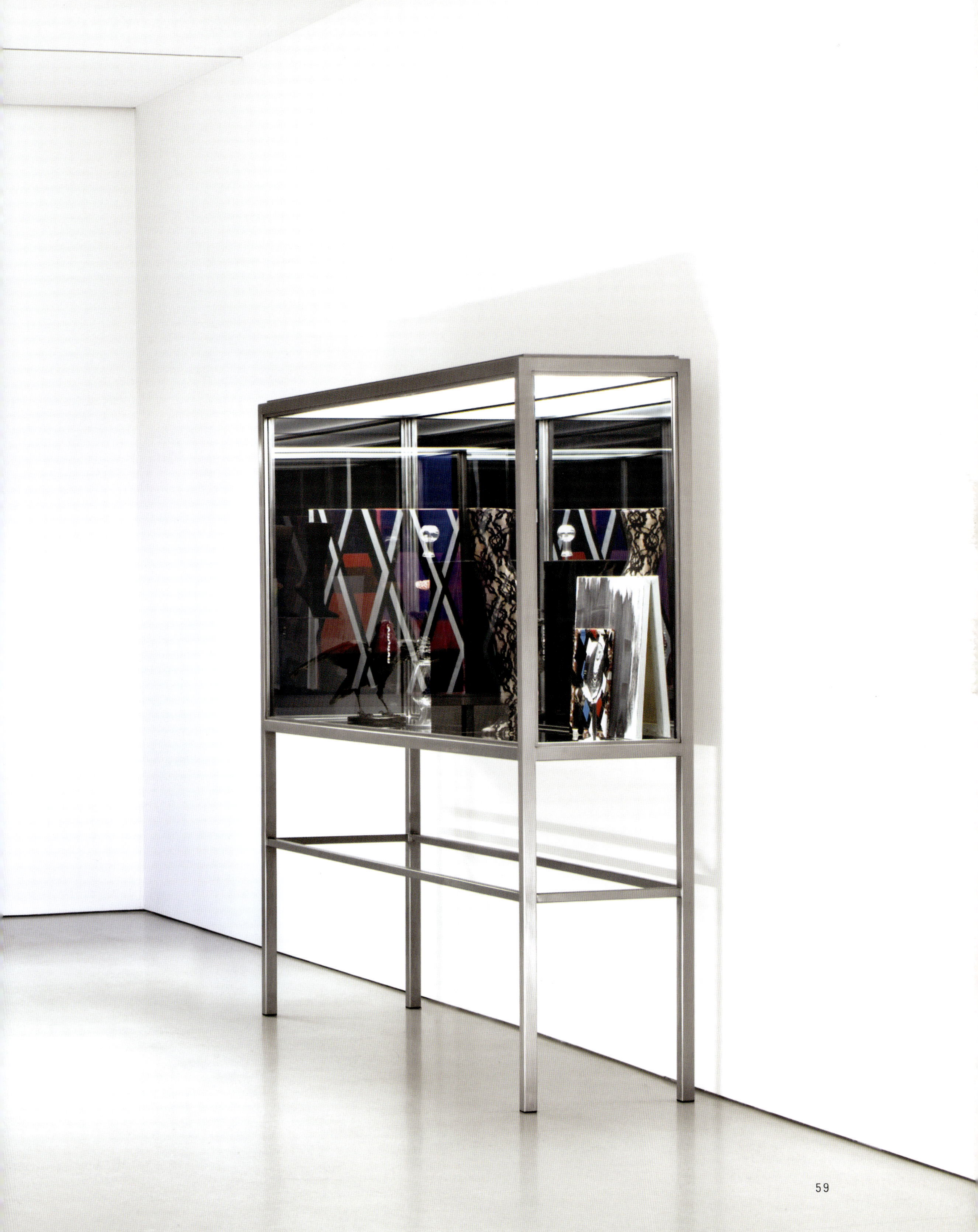

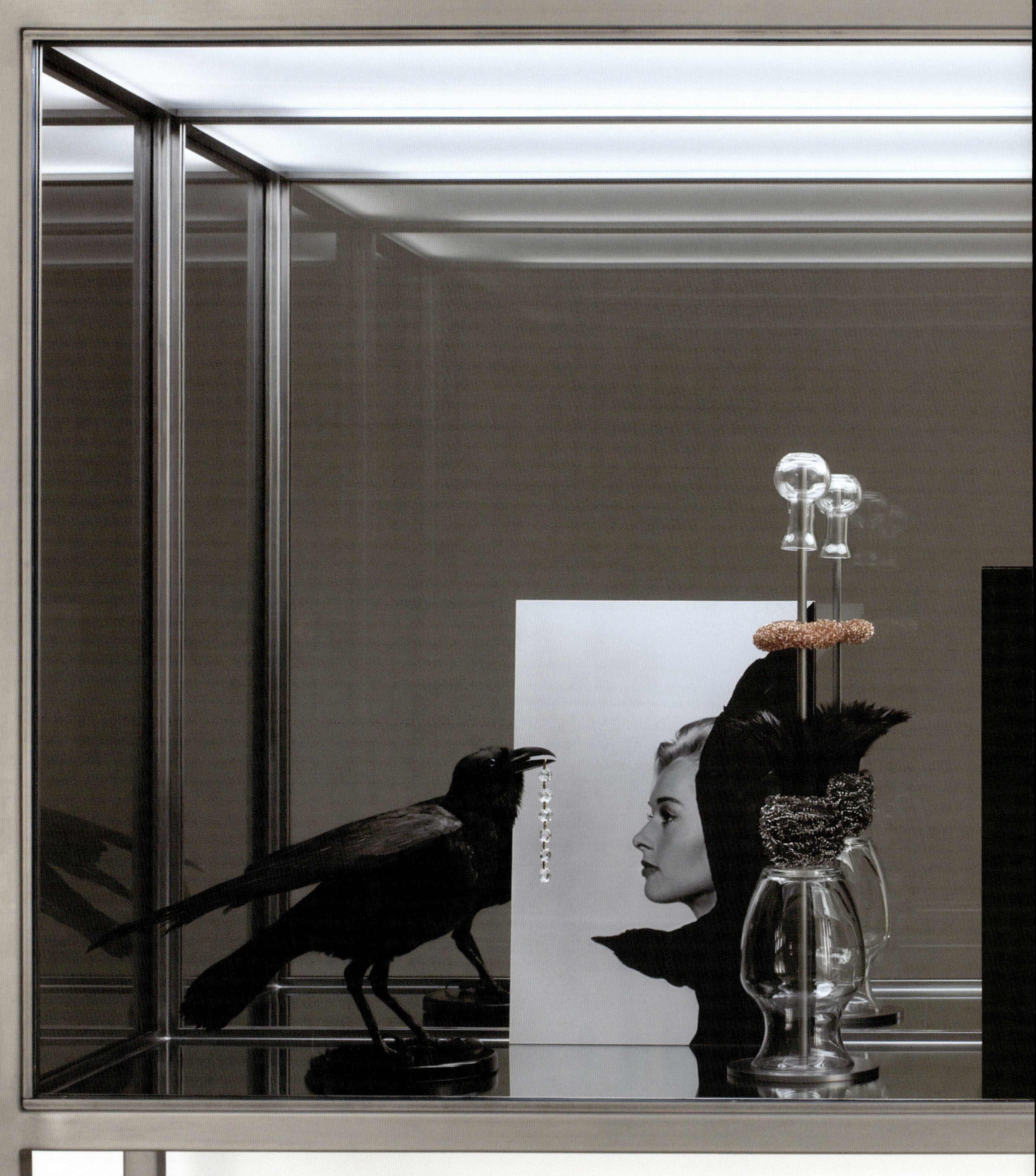

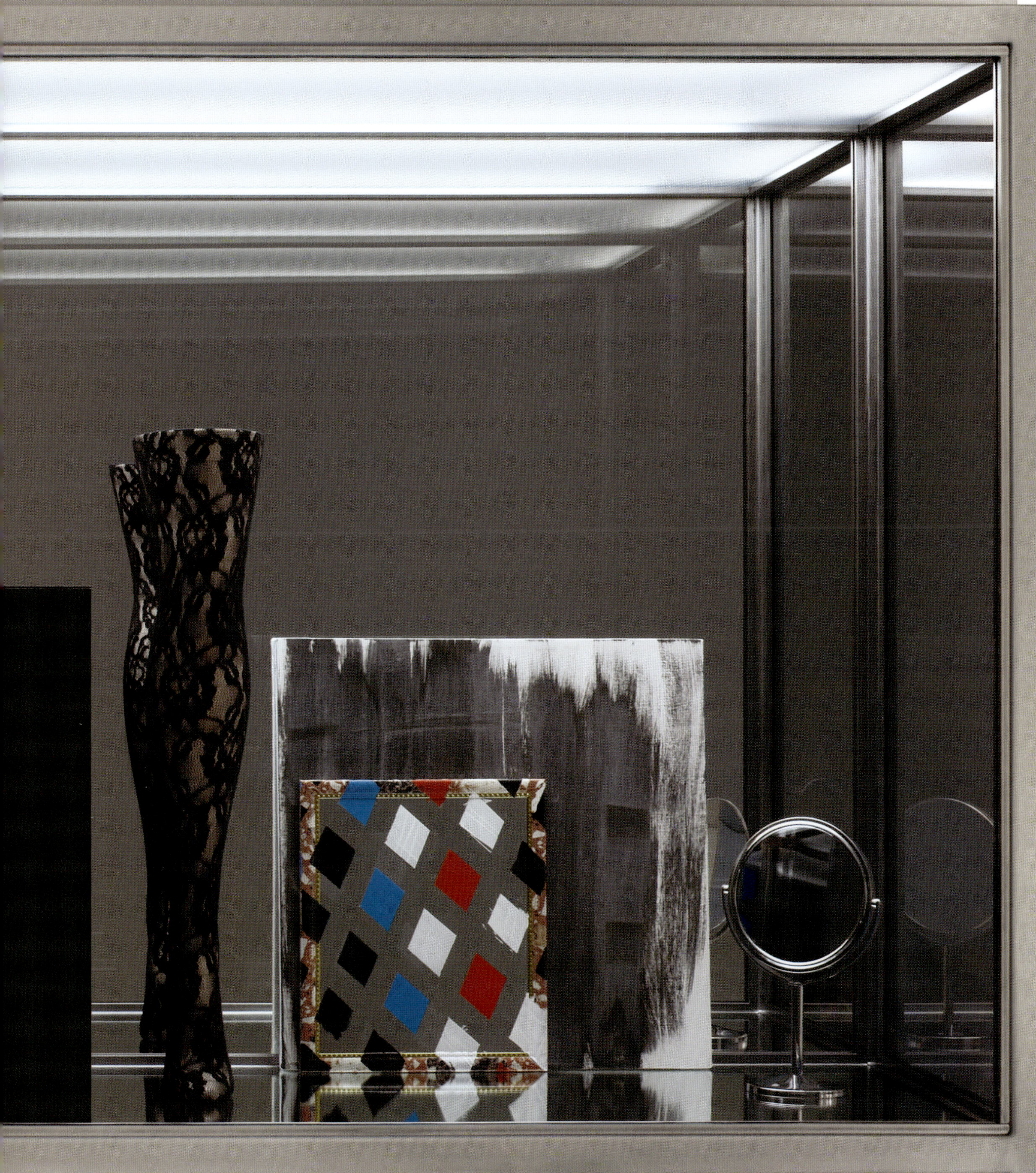

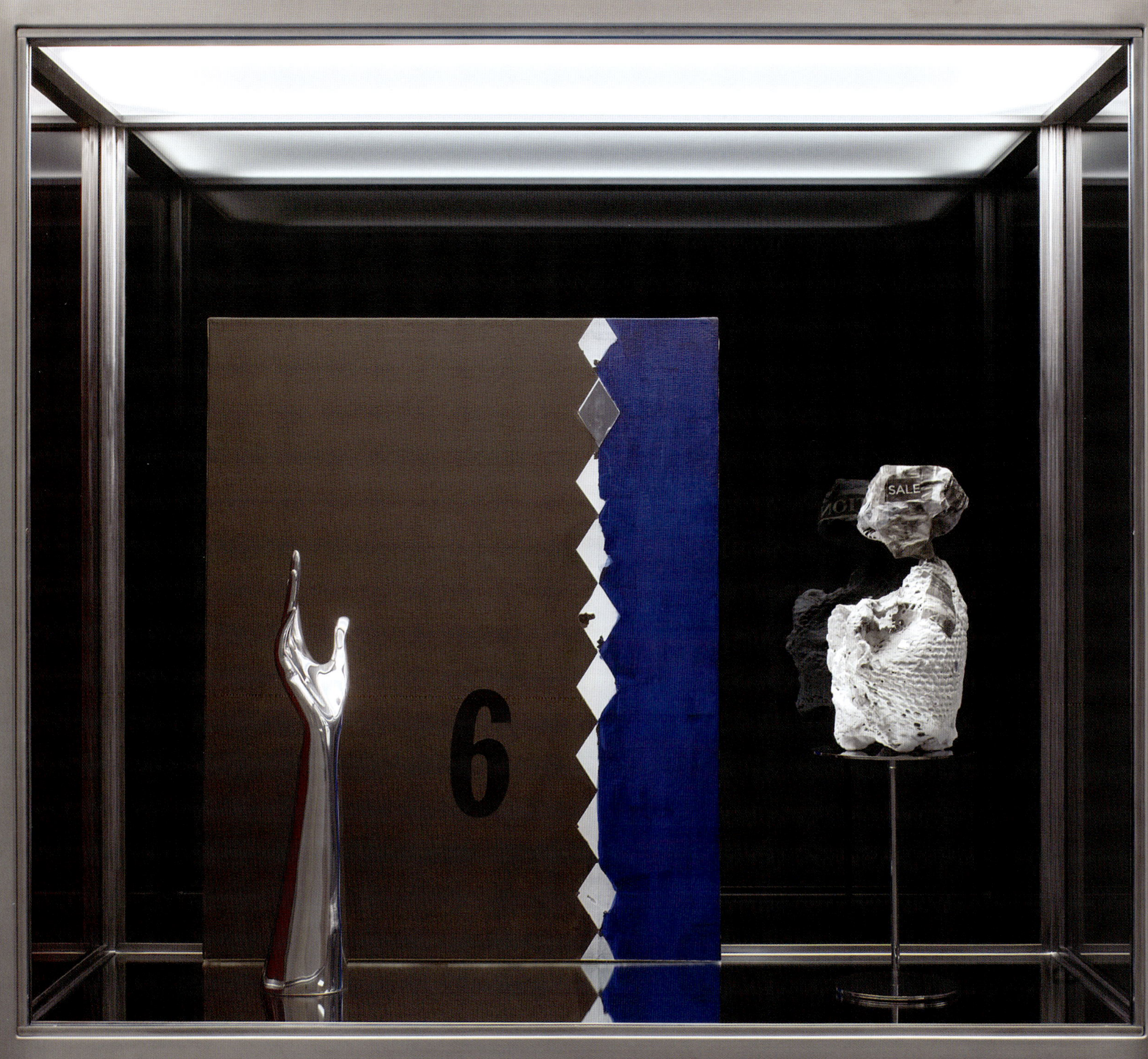
6
SALE

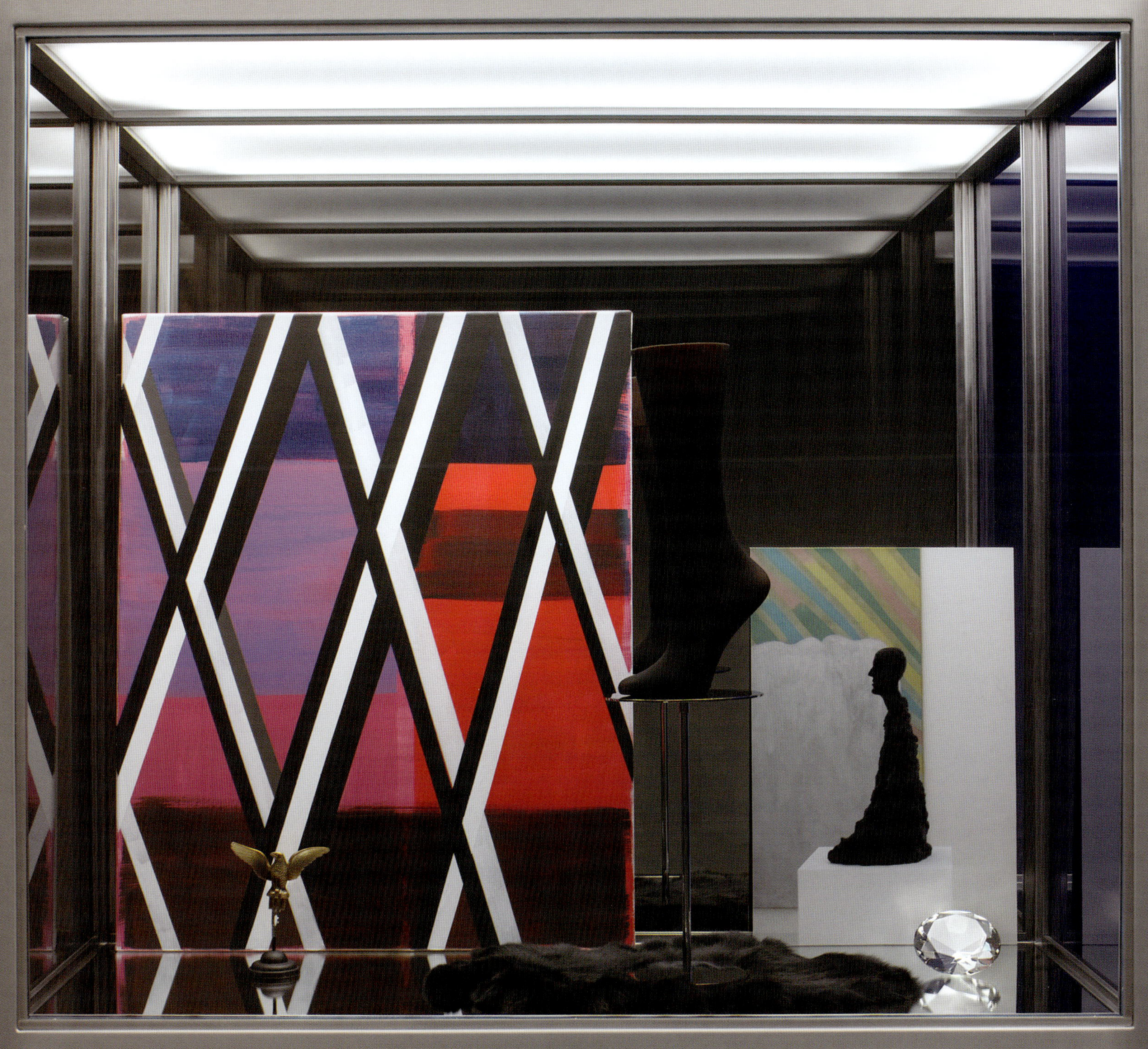

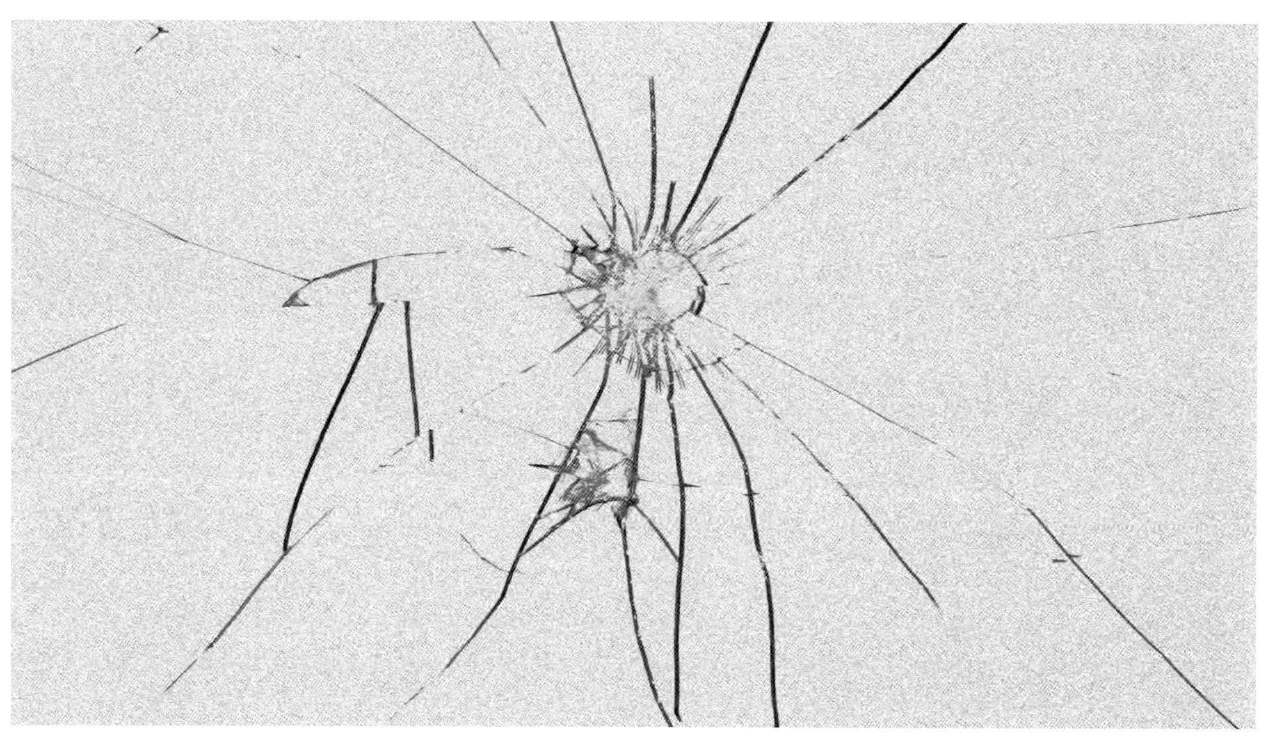

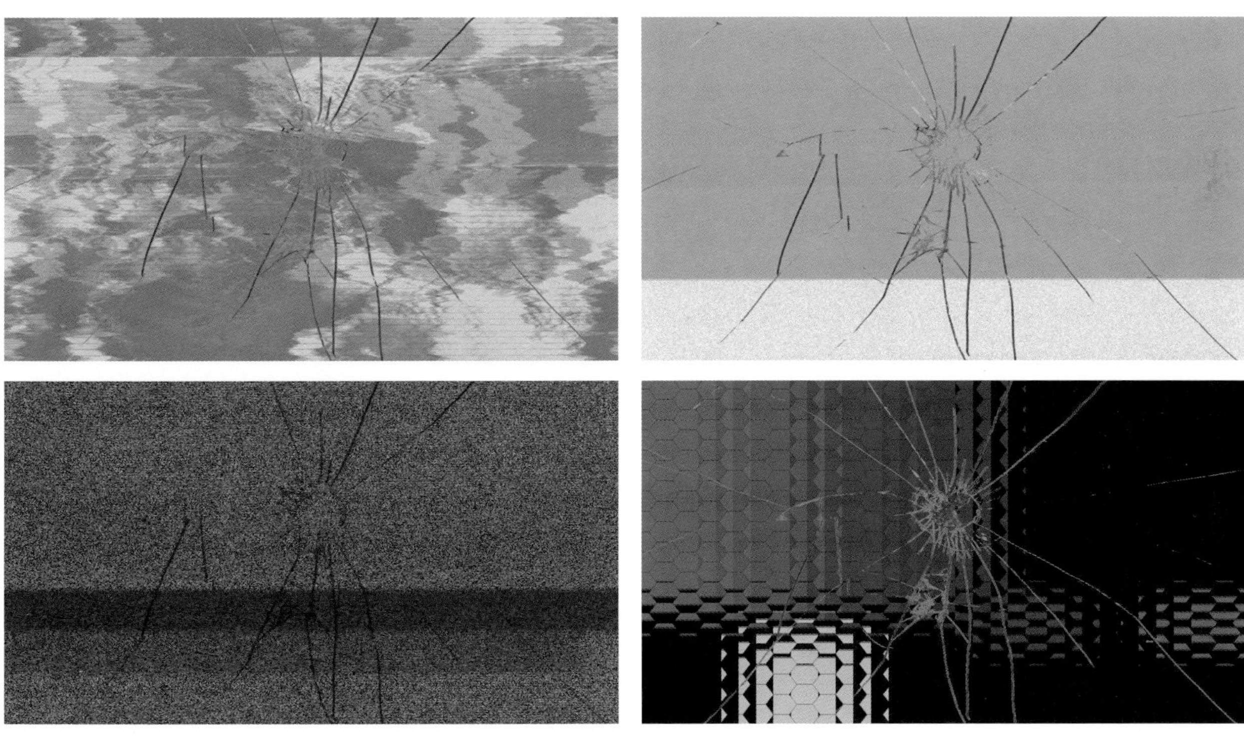

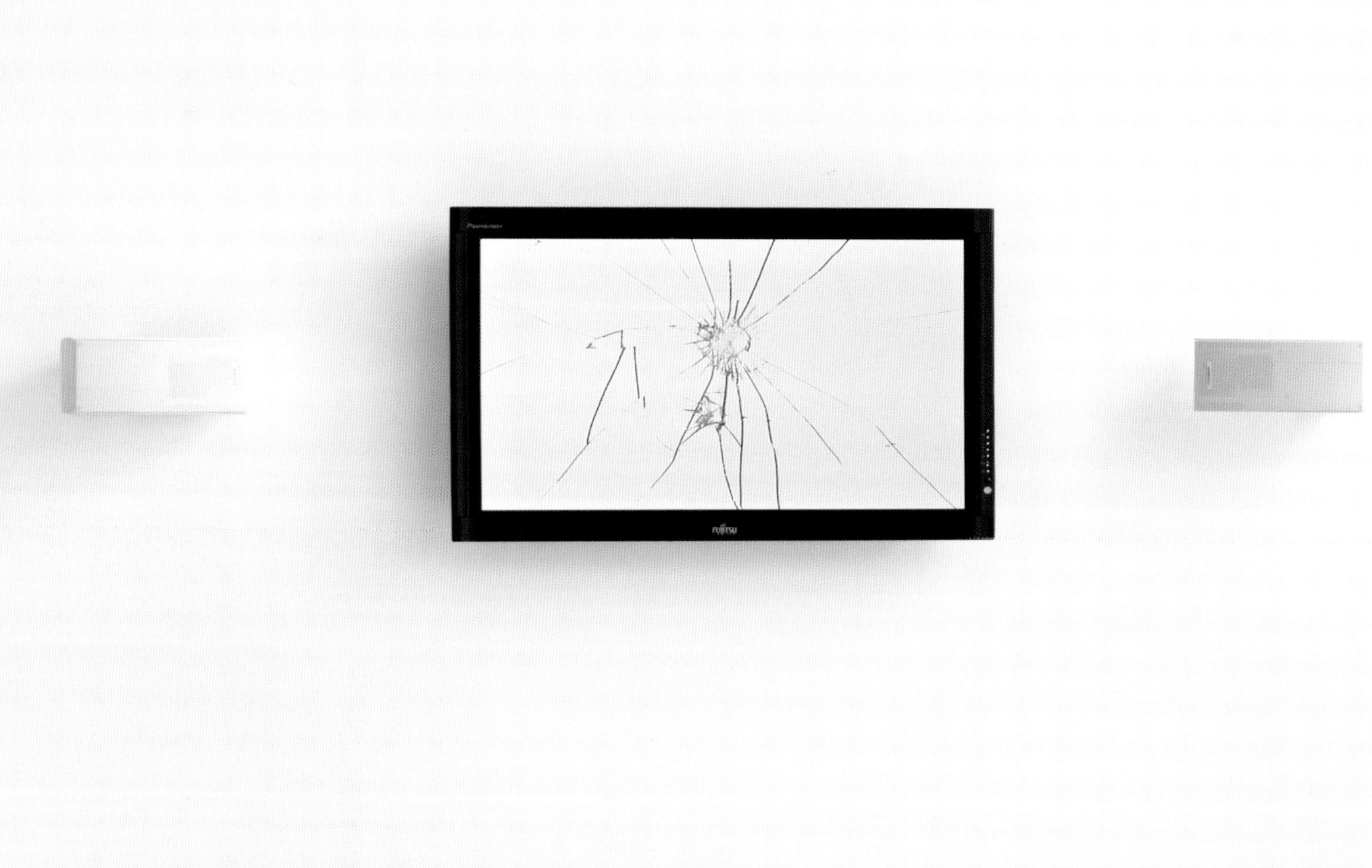

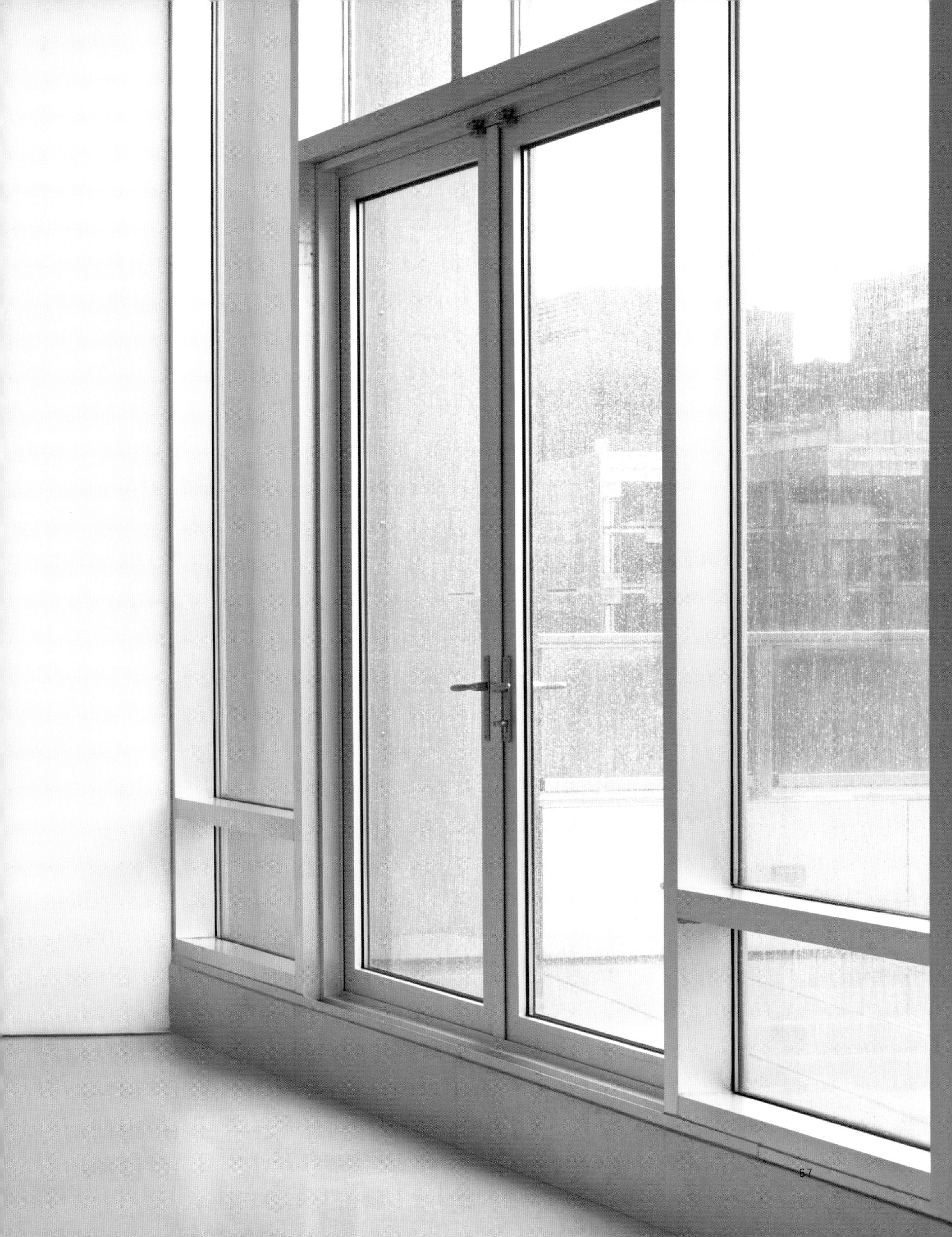

JOSEPHINE MECKSEPER

Meckseper received her MFA from the California Institute of the Arts (1992). Her works have been included in international biennials such as *Prospect.1 New Orleans* (2008); the Second Moscow Biennale of Contemporary Art (2007); the Second Biennial of Contemporary Art of Seville (2006); the Seventy-third Whitney Biennial: *Day for Night* (2006); and the Eighth Biennale d'Art Contemporain de Lyon: *Experiencing Duration* (2005). Her work was exhibited in *Resistance Is* at the Whitney Museum of American Art in New York (2007), and in *Media Burn* at the Tate Modern and *USA Today* at the Royal Academy of Arts in London (both in 2006). She has also had solo exhibitions at Gesellschaft für Aktuelle Kunst, Bremen (2008); the Migros Museum für Gegenwartskunst, Zurich; Ausstellungshalle zeitgenössische Kunst, Münster; and the Blaffer Gallery/Art Museum of the University of Houston (2009). She was the subject of a retrospective at the Kunstmuseum Stuttgart (2007). Her work was featured at the Museum of Modern Art in *New Photography* (2008) and in *Contemplating the Void* at the Solomon R. Guggenheim Museum, New York (2010), and was recently on view at the Seventy-fifth Whitney Biennial (2010). Her work is included in the Tenth Sharjah Biennial: *Plot for a Biennial* (2011).

LIST OF WORKS

ABOUT THE AUTHORS

FRANCESCO BONAMI is the artistic director of the Fondazione Sandretto in Turin, Italy, and the chief editor of *Tar Magazine.* He was the director of the Fiftieth Venice Biennale (2003) and the curator of the Seventy-fifth Whitney Biennial (2010). Bonami recently curated Rudolf Stingel's show at Gagosian Gallery in New York. He is a board member of the Swiss Institute in New York.

JOHN CASSIDY has been a staff writer at *The New Yorker* since 1995. Cassidy is also a contributor to The New York Review of Books and a financial commentator for the BBC. His latest book, *How Markets Fail: The Logic of Economic Calamities,* was published in November, 2009, by Farrar, Straus and Giroux.

JAMES FREY is from Cleveland. He has written four books, all international best sellers, and texts for artists such as Richard Prince, Ed Ruscha, Damien Hirst, and Richard Phillips. His work is published in thirty-nine languages.

STEPHEN ROACH, a member of the faculty of Yale University, is also Non-Executive Chairman of Morgan Stanley Asia and author of *The Next Asia* (Wiley 2009). From 1982 to 2007, he was Morgan Stanley's Senior and Chief Economist.

ACKNOWLEDGEMENTS

THE ARTIST WISHES TO THANK

Glenn Fuhrman
Amanda Fuhrman
Stephanie Roach
Rebecca Streiman
Arianna Petrich
John Martin Widger
Cynthia Daignault
Zachary Zahringer
David Shull
Hsiao Chen
Vallessa Monk
Clif Hawkins

Francesco Bonami
John Cassidy
James Frey
Stephen Roach
Richard Phillips
Genevieve Hanson
Amy Mees
Michael Vaden's Wildlife Artistry
Greenberg Display
ARNDT, Berlin
Elizabeth Dee, New York
Timothy Taylor Gallery, London

THE FLAG ART FOUNDATION WISHES TO THANK

Josephine Meckseper for her brilliant vision and the stunning and thought-provoking works that so beautifully fill the space.

Marian Goodman and Gerhard Richter for helping us borrow and install such an incredible juxtaposition to Josephine's work. Steve Griffin for his guidance during installation.

Jamie Forehand, Beto Hopper, Ryan Edward Muller, and Jonathan Andrews
of Acumen Fine Art Logistics

Margaret Knowles, Suzannah Gerber, and Eumi Lee of The FLAG Art Foundation

Rebecca Streiman of The FLAG Art Foundation

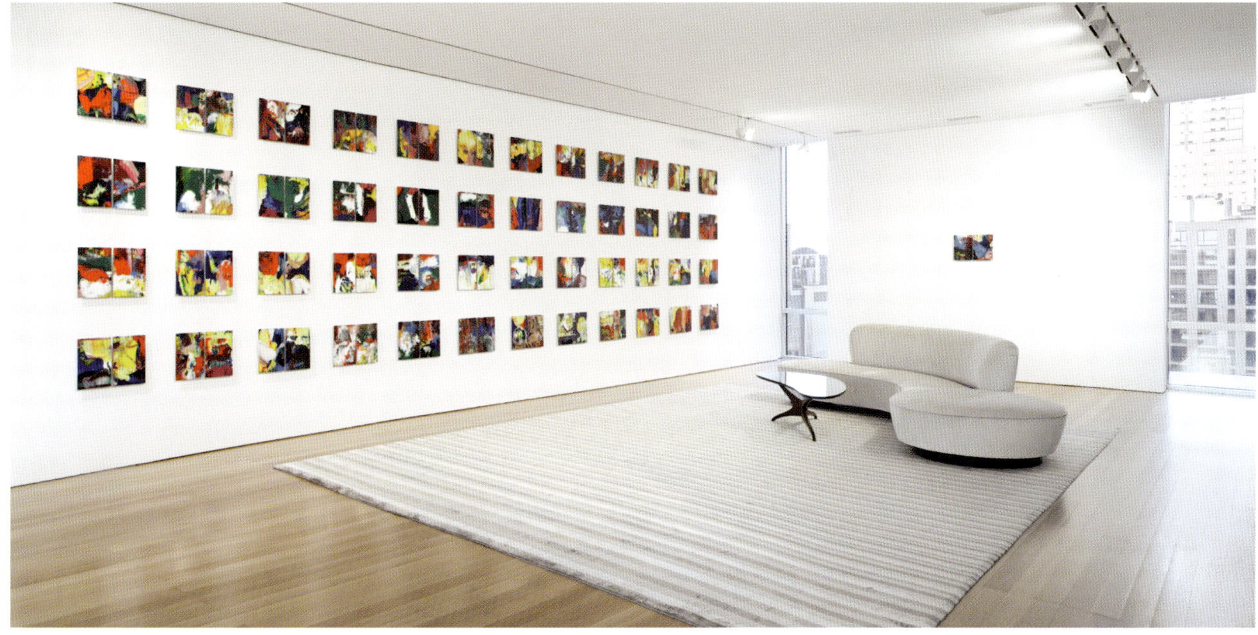

Installation view of *Sinbad,* 2008, by Gerhard Richter on the 10th floor of
The FLAG Art Foundation during the Josephine Meckseper exhibition in the 9th floor galleries.

The FLAG Art Foundation is an exhibition space for contemporary art. The program includes three to five professionally curated shows per year. Each consists of works by established and emerging international artists. We are located on the 9th and 10th floors of the Chelsea Arts Tower in the heart of New York's art district on 25th Street between 10th and 11th Avenues.

Our objective is to encourage the appreciation of contemporary art among a diverse audience. FLAG provides a unique educational environment in which visitors can view, contemplate, and engage in active dialogue with the artworks. Curators select and borrow from a variety of sources to include a wide range of work in each exhibition. FLAG is also a resource that facilitates loans of contemporary artworks to museums around the world.

Stephanie Roach, Director of The FLAG Art Foundation
All interior images photographed by Genevieve Hanson
Book design by Amy Mees, X-ing Design